Poetspeak:
In their work, about their work

Poetspeak:

In their work, about their work

A selection by Paul B. Janeczko

BRADBURY PRESS   NEW YORK

Every book is the work of more than one person. But an anthology would not be possible without the work and energy of a lot of people. These people deserve my thanks.

First of all, I must thank all the poets who gave so freely of their time, effort, and art. Dealing with these men and women was a gratifying experience. I am especially indebted to seven contributors: Ted Kooser, William Stafford, Robert Wallace, Peter Wild, Keith Wilson, Mark Vinz, and Paul Zimmer. These poets gladly sent me material when *Poetspeak* was only an idea. When I wasn't sure if the idea would fly, their work made it soar.

My sister, Mary, risked bags under her eyes getting to work early to make copies of the manuscript.

My brother, Mark, while not risking (or caring) about bags under his eyes, claims he risked his job making copies of the manuscript.

Nadine deserves my thanks for a lot of things, but in this case for the title of the book, and for putting up with piles of poems and a kitchen table that too often served as my second desk.

Finally, I must thank Richard Jackson, my editor at Bradbury Press. He has believed in me and my work from the very beginning. I value his editorial advice. I treasure his friendship.   —*P.B.J.*

Copyright © 1983 by Paul B. Janeczko. Pages 230 – 236 constitute an extension of the copyright page.

Bradbury Press
An affiliate of Macmillan, Inc.
866 Third Avenue, New York, NY 10022
Collier Macmillan Canada, Inc.
Manufactured in the United States of America
10 9 8 7 6 5
The text of this book is set in 11 pt. Sabon.
Library of Congress Cataloging in Publication Data
Main entry under title:
Poetspeak: in their work, about their work.
   Includes index.
   Summary: A collection of 148 poems on a variety of topics by 62 modern poets who provide commentary on their individual works.
   1. American poetry — 20th century. 2. American poetry — Collections
I. Janeczko, Paul B.
PS593.C45P63   1983   811'.54'08   83-2715
ISBN 0-02-747770-3

For Peter Berry,
friend and main man,
with love
and all that jazz

Contents

x

Gregory Corso

Richard Wilbur
Photo: Rhoda Nathans

Richard Snyder

Nikki Giovanni

Greg Kuzma

Ted Kooser
Photo: William Stafford

David Allan Evans

Jonathan Holden

Thom Gunn
Photo: Bill Schuessler

Doug Cockrell

Robert Currie

William Matthews

oward Nemerov
oto: Herb Weitman

William Dickey

Richard Eberhart

Maxine Kumin
Photo: Kelly Wise

Barbara Howes

Mark Vinz
Photo: Wayne Gudmundson

Roy Scheele
Photo: Judy Seward

Cynthia
Macdonald

X.J. Kennedy

The poets pictured are those who were able
to provide photographs for *Poetspeak.*—P.B.J.

Ralph Pomeroy

Don Welch

Philip Booth
Photo:
Camera North

Stanley Kunitz
Photo: Renate Ponsold

Paul Zimmer

Gary Gildner

William Stafford
Photo:
Barbara Stafford

Richard Shelton
Photo:
David L. Hudnall

Philip Dacey

William Jay Smith

Mike Lowery

Henry Carlile
Photo: Sandra McPherson

Celeste Turner Wright

Linda Pastan
Photo: Thomas Victor

Phil Hey
Photo: H. Payer

Robert Wallace

Peter Meinke

Frank Steele

Vern Rutsala
Photo: Joan Rutsala

Joyce Carol Oates
Photo: Jerry Bauer

Ed Ochester

Edward Field

Sam Cornish

Paul Zimmer:
WHAT ZIMMER WOULD BE

When asked, I used to say,
"I want to be a doctor."
Which is the same thing
As a child saying,
"I want to be a priest,"
Or
"I want to be a magician,"
Which is the laying
Of hands, the vibrations,
The rabbit in the hat,
Or the body in the cup,
The curing of the sick
And the raising of the dead.

"Fix and fix, you're all better,"
I would say
To the neighborhood wounded
As we fought the world war
Through the vacant lots of Ohio.
"Fix and fix, you're all better,"
And they would rise
To fight again.
                    But then
I saw my aunt die slowly of cancer
And a man struck down by a car.

All along I had really
Wanted to be a poet,
Which is, you see, almost
The same thing as saying,
"I want to be a doctor,"
"I want to be a priest,"

1

Or
"I want to be a magician."
All along, without realizing it,
I had wanted to be a poet.

Fix and fix, you're all better.

✍ I would like to make a few comments on how I came to make the poem, "What Zimmer Would Be." There is a period when very young children begin to ask each other the question, "What are you going to be when you grow up?" Later it becomes an even more serious matter when parents and teachers begin asking the same question. I was never very good at school. I can recall many occasions when my teacher nuns would call my parents into school and tell them that the reason I wasn't doing well in class was that I was a "dreamer." I always thought that being a dreamer was a neat thing to be. In fact, I still do. But at that time it was a problem for me. As I experienced my failures, the question continued to plague me. What *was* I going to do with my life? I devised a way of silencing my questioners. I always said that I wanted to be a doctor. That impressed everyone very much and usually ended the conversation. But I never really knew.

I made this poem in remembrance of that time. It would be helpful for you to know a couple of things about the imagery in the poem. When I was growing up in Ohio, World War II was in progress. In my neighborhood we children would imitate the world by pretending war. We would choose up sides and fight great battles with our play guns. I always played the combat doctor in these games because . . . well, I was going to *be* a doctor. Some of the imagery from this experience appears in the middle of the poem. The reason I say that I want to be a priest or a magician is because these were the other two hot items on my career list as a kid. Of course I never really knew I wanted to be a poet. In fact, as I recall, I doubt if I even knew what a poet was. I am glad I found out. I believe I had early subconscious yearnings toward the craft. That was what the dreaming was about.   —P.Z.

Peter Meinke:
ADVICE TO MY SON

The trick is, to live your days
as if each one may be your last
(for they go fast, and young men lose their lives
in strange and unimaginable ways)
but at the same time, plan long range
(for they go slow: if you survive
the shattered windshield and the bursting shell
you will arrive
at our approximation here below
of heaven or hell).

To be specific, between the peony and the rose
plant squash and spinach, turnips and tomatoes;
beauty is nectar
and nectar, in a desert, saves—
but the stomach craves stronger sustenance
than the honied vine.
Therefore, marry a pretty girl
after seeing her mother;
speak truth to one man,
work with another;
and always serve bread with your wine.

But, son,
always serve wine.

William Dickey:
TUTANKHAMEN

In a museum, I ask
what is the one thing
I would most want to steal?

It could be and has,
something as enormous
as *La Grande Jatte,*
with all of the
preliminary sketches.

Here it is only
an alabaster lion
with a red tongue.
Is it a lion
standing up,
asking for sweetmeats?
Is it a lion
that has been
trained to dance?

Sweating, plugged into
the usual earphone,
the crowd clots about
gold, gold.
Gold and lapis,
but it is the gold
that really matters.

All of them,
the antique blue ladies,
my friend in the wheelchair,
are they looking in

at themselves
through that ornate mask?

If they are
I will skid
rapidly into the next gallery.
Nobody will be watching.

I will pick up the lion,
my size of lion,
with the red tongue.
I will make off with him.

Steal what you want,
not what the catalogue
says you ought to.

Marge Piercy:
FOR THE YOUNG WHO WANT TO

Talent is what they say
you have after the novel
is published and favorably
reviewed. Beforehand what
you have is a tedious
delusion, a hobby like knitting.

Work is what you have done
after the play is produced
and the audience claps.
Before that friends keep asking
when you are planning to go
out and get a job.

Genius is what they know you
had after the third volume
of remarkable poems. Earlier
they accuse you of withdrawing,
ask why you don't have a baby,
call you a bum.

The reason people want M.F.A.'s,
take workshops with fancy names
when all you can really
learn is a few techniques,
typing instructions and somebody else's mannerisms

is that every artist lacks
a license to hang on the wall
like your optician, your vet
proving you may be a clumsy sadist
whose fillings fall into the stew
but you're certified a dentist.

The real writer is one
who really writes. Talent
is an invention like phlogiston
after the fact of fire.
Work is its own cure. You have to
like it better than being loved.

X.J. Kennedy:
KEEP A HAND ON YOUR DREAM

Keep a hand on your dream—
  Let it go too soon
And, though broad in the beam
  As a blown balloon,

It will dart all around
  Taking crazy trips,
Blowing spittle and sound
  From insulting lips.

Maxine Kumin:
FRÄULEIN READS INSTRUCTIVE RHYMES

Outside Help for Parents Who May Have Forgotten "Der Struwelpeter" by Heinrich Hoffmann

First hear the story of Kaspar the rosy-cheeked.
Once he was round and fat. He ate his dinner up.
Then, see, on Monday night, nothing will Kaspar eat.
Tuesday and Wednesday, *nein!* Kaspar throws down his cup.
Watch him shrink to a stick crying *nicht!* all that week.
Sunday he whispers *nicht* and falls down dead.
Now they must bury him. In the black earth he's meek.
And by his grave they leave Kaspar his meat and bread.
  Therefore, says Fräulein, slicing the sauerbraten,
  eat what I fix for you. See what can happen?

Next prances Friedrich the terrible-tempered.
He pulls the wings from flies.
He wrings the chickens' necks.
See with a long horsewhip how in this picture he

lashes the maid who cries into her handkerchief.
Wait, *aber*, all is well. Here the big dog comes in.
Angry black dog bites his knee and holds fast.
Now the Herr Doktor pours Friedrich bad medicine.
Downstairs, the napkined dog eats Friedrich's liverwurst.
  Child, says Fräulein, clicking her thimble cup,
  good, *ja*, be good, or the dog comes to eat you up.

Now look at Konrad the little thumb-sucker.
Ach, but his poor mama cries when she warns him
the tailor will come for his thumbs if he sucks them.
Quick he can cut them off, easy as paper.
Out goes the mother and *wupp!* goes the thumbkin in.
Then the door opens. Enter the tailor.
See in the picture the terrible tongue in
his grinning red mouth! In his hands the great shears.
Just as she told him, the tailor goes *klipp und klapp*.
Eight-fingered Konrad has learned a sad lesson.
  Therefore, says Fräulein, shaking her chignon,
  suck you must not or the tailor will chop!

Here is smart Robert the flying boy, bad one.
Hui! How the storm blows and coughs in the treetops.
Mama has told him today he must stay in,
but Robert slips out with umbrella and rain cap.
Now he is flying. The wind sucks and pulls him.
See, he is carried up, smaller and smaller.
His cap flies ahead of him, no one can help him.
  Therefore, says Fräulein, smoothing her collar,
  mind me, says Fräulein. God stands up in Heaven.
  See how He watches? He snatches the bad ones.

☙ "Fräulein Reads Instructive Rhymes" was written very
early in my life-experience as poet. It came up directly from
my childhood memory, for the little stories in the poem are

9

adaptations from a German children's book that was read to me, and that marked me forever. That book, *Der Struwelpeter,* or *Slovenly Peter,* is full of nasty moral tales that were designed to terrify children into behaving themselves. For example, on one page we read about a little girl who plays with matches; we turn the page and there she is, burning to death. The poem makes fun of the admonitions but at the same time recognizes the terrible force they have. It was my plan to build from one moral lesson to another, ending with the most awesome. But in truth audiences always seem more affected by the thumb-sucking story than any of the others. Apparently all of us were thumb-suckers and still harbor some guilty feelings about this practice. Nobody today seems very afraid of being carried off in the sky, which was my biggest fear.

Technically, the poem tries to imitate a kind of singsong rhythm, the doggerel line of the original German. It uses rhyme and strong meter, but most of all it uses vivid, concrete detail to involve the reader in each evil little event.

Fräulein is the nursemaid, or babysitter. The poem wants to be understood as heavily satirical.   —*M.K.*

Gregory Corso:
I MET THIS GUY WHO DIED
—*for J.L.K.*

We caroused
    did the bars
        became fast friends
He wanted me to tell him
    what poetry was
        I told him

Happy tipsy one night
I took him home to see my newborn child
A great sorrow overcame him
"O Gregory" he moaned
    "you brought up something to die"

 The title is what I call high-class because did I meet a guy who died and came back to life, or did I meet a guy who died after I knew him? Titles are *so* important in poesy.

He told me the truth—a shocking one, true, but a great honest shot. When he asked me to tell him what poetry was, and I say:

I told him

Enough—I didn't have to go into detail—it would have screwed up the poem. Poems are best delivered fast, sharp, smart and tellingly. They can help you realize something you could not understand before—they can illuminate the spirit with long forgotten beauties and uglies—

Poetry is a true God-gift to humankind, also poetry is the opposite of hypocrisy.　　　　　　　—G.C.

David Ignatow:
THE JOURNEY

I am looking for a past
I can rely on
in order to look to death
with equanimity.
What was given me:
my mother's largeness
to protect me,
my father's regularity
in coming home from work
at night, his opening the door
silently and smiling,
pleased to be back
and the lights on
in all the rooms
through which I could run
freely or sit at ease
at table and do my homework
undisturbed: love arranged
as order directed at the next day.
Going to bed was a journey.

∝ "The Journey" was written in recollection of a period in my childhood when things at home and in the street and school were going well, without painful problems. It was a lovely period which in my mature years I began to appreciate as a key period in my life, giving me a way of life to work towards in my maturity. It was a signpost during the turmoil I was confronted with as an adult in politics, in business, and in domestic affairs. I could look back at that relatively calm and relaxed time as a goal to work towards in my adult life and as a kind of saving vision to keep me from becoming altogether despairing.

Notice that the writing has a kind of nostalgia towards the end of the poem and that the poem begins with a backward look and statement of need in midst of a barely disguised longing for death, which, as the poem progresses, becomes transformed into a celebration of peace and hope, the longing for death absorbed in the vision of the beautiful past.   —D.I.

Vern Rutsala:
THE WAR OF THE WORLDS

So many things happen
on trips yet all we
remember is middle—
start and finish burned
away, lost like pencil
points and erasers.
But this is okay.
Memory lights up
that old stretch of road
and I feel the rough
upholstery of my back
seat corner. They've turned
on the radio and I hear
the invaders advance on
Princeton, New Jersey—
a place much farther than
Mars—hear the speaker
conjure the pylon shadow
with panic, then
the spitting sound
of things being crushed
followed by silence,
that beautiful ominous
silence yawning all the way

to Idaho and filling
our small car with echoes.
I feel very calm
and invisible. The world
is more interesting
than I had been led
to believe. I think we'll
survive—they never mention
Idaho on the radio.
And there are no shadows,
only green hills and meadows
and the men's airless calm—
my father and his friend
saying "war" with proper
respect, my mother calm
and interested too,
but the other woman
suddenly hysterical, crying:
"My babies! My babies!"
Childhood's usual embarrassed
witness I am sad at this
and concentrate politely
on the view, pleased
with my insignificance
and sure no invasion is worth
such tears and foolishness.

ᙚ "The War of the Worlds" refers to the radio broadcast
Orson Welles made in 1938. The event is seen from the perspective of a child. What happens in the poem is very close to
what I remember of that day.   —V.R.

Peter Wild:
AIR RAID

I imagined the bombs and fighters
crashing in our woods
where we'd find them the next day,
perhaps scare a prisoner out of
the brambles where the pheasants lived
into farmer Loomis' yard where
at last chasing him around the house
he'd give up half starved, repentant,
arms raised. my fat aunts giggled
as they moved through the house pulling shades,
and my father went into the cellar
to turn down the furnace, came
clomping back up the stairs with
a fist of candles, one lit leading the way.
and so we sat not knowing what to do with it,
remembering stories about the submarines
landing where the Pilgrims had, before
slipping back releasing their men into the moonlit
landscape of the continent, who by day
walked among us speaking perfect English,
took jobs as carpenters, made friends with children,
and who someone said lived in a shack
hidden out on the pine barrens sending
their secrets back across the ocean.
I wondered how they got enough sleep
working both night and day, hugged
the bewildered dog whose shadows
kept escaping from my arms, and
someone hushed us with a finger
as if we might be heard, and we listened
        as in a minute one long plane
groaned overhead into its path of lights

going dim across New England, and a moment later
my father pulled the curtains back
to Mr. Graham, the town's coal man, still
in his pajamas, wearing his World War One helmet
standing there tapping at the window, and
my father nodding back as I saw
him looking up, say to us "All clear. All clear."

∽ I'm just old enough to remember the air-raid warnings
during World War II. The poem is a memory of those nights
when we heard the bell tolling from the tower of the old brick
firehouse, and we, with the other families in our rural New
England town, dutifully pulled the shades and dimmed our
lights.

I'm among those who hold that life is one thing, art is another—verisimilitude is not art. On the surface, "Air Raid" is
a near journalistic account of a scene in which little happens
outwardly. Accurate down to the details: Mr. Graham was our
local coal man, and I can still see him gaping at the window.

Yet sitting in the near dark with the dog and the family as
an airplane—possibly an enemy airplane—drones over, is a
spooky thing, a potentially exciting thing, for a youngster. He
doesn't know whether to giggle or pray. Rich ground for myth
to creep in and take root, an excursion into fantasy relieved by
the ending of the poem. And I guess that is what much of life,
and much of poetry, is about.

And there is irony, too. For there were no enemy planes
flying over, dropping bombs, killing people as they were then
doing across Europe—but the possibility provided a thrill
without danger, and in the poem, I think, a window into an
inner landscape.   —P.W.

Judith Hemschemeyer:
THE PAINTERS

Everything was yellow:
the warm, milk-yellow paint
they got by mixing in the white
and stirring it with long, flat wooden sticks,

the lemonade she made
and gave to me to take to them
in the white enamel pitcher rimmed with blue,

the ropes of piss they pissed into the paint . . .
"Did not!"
"Did too!" I told my sister.
"They said it makes the paint *adhere.*"

"Those two!" Mother laughed when we told her,
and she blushed and made more lemonade.
We'd never seen her so happy, joking with them,

her arm flung over her face for shade.
And by supper the house was yellow too,
our wooden cave sealed thick and tight and safe
with paint and piss and lemonade.

◦◦◦ I think I wrote this poem because I was nostalgic for my
childhood, especially for the good days.

Nothing is "made up." Everything is remembered. But not
until I got the first line, "Everything was yellow," was I able
to write the poem. That's because every poem has to have an
organizing principle. The statement "Everything was yellow"
gave me my structure. Of course everything *wasn't* yellow; the
pitcher was white rimmed with blue, the grass was green, etc.

But the poet exaggerates, bends the scene to conform to her intense recollection of it. Sometimes it works!

There is no formal rhyme scheme here, but there are lots of similar sounds: shade, made, lemonade; adhere, her, sister; too, blue, two.

P.S. I got the first line when I was sitting in a friend's backyard. Her house is yellow too, and suddenly I remembered the day forty years before, that our house had been painted. –*J.H.*

Philip Dacey:
PRISMS (Altea)

It was a rainbow impossibly
beautiful, straddling the town
with one foot poised lightly on the sea

and the other set atop the mountain
behind us. It was a fairy-tale
rainbow if there ever was one.

For days rain had made a jail
of the world, but now Emmett and I
were out walking; when we stopped to marvel

at the banded color and he asked, Why
are there rainbows? I explained how water,
a prism, builds archways in the sky.

Days later, as we sat together
in the plaza, each with paper and pen
to write or draw, Emmett's clear

plastic ballpoint bent the sunlight into a rainbow on his wrist.
We both laughed: it was small and thin

but there it was. Who could have guessed
prisms wait in disguise right under
our noses, that when you least

expect it a prism will appear,
breaking the light to show its color?

In 1975 I spent six months in Spain with my wife and children. This poem came out of that experience. It's a poem that definitely leads to a climax the way jokes have a punchline. The reason-for-being of jokes is their punchlines. In a similar way the value of this poem rests upon its conclusion, the idea that prisms can unexpectedly appear anywhere. I don't mean that idea to be a tacked-on moral, of course, but to be an idea that grows out of the poem's narrative, that seems a necessary development, not something imposed by me on the material. The prism is a metaphor and represents any surprising events in our lives that provide us with important revelations. The word "breaking" suggests some of these events might be painful. The verse-form used is terza rima, which means the lines rhyme aba, bcb, cdc, etc. The challenge in writing in terza rima, which is quite artificial and arbitrary, is to make the writing seem natural. I like the poem because I feel I've met that challenge successfully; I also like it because I believe in the importance of the poem's main idea.   —P.D.

Ed Ochester:
110 YEAR OLD HOUSE

Betsy, if pencil erasers could sing
they'd sound like your finches,

the only birds I've seen that seem
to like being caged, in their little pagoda

croaking like miniature geese
to the Jackson Browne that Ned's taping

for his report on strip mines
and to the sound of the grackles

that live in the attic.
To them, everything's music.

And to me, snoozing with my flu,
watching the machines crawl the strip mine

in back of the Schmeltzers';
I'm so lazy today even the muffled thump

of the miners' dynamite
and the rattling of the loose window make sense

and you most of all, yelling in the kitchen
"my finches, I must say hello to my finches"

and running up the stairs
with your 11 year old feet

so hard that the whole old house trembles
and then the slam of your door

and a chorus of finch honks which, as you say
"is just their way of saying hello"

to you, to us, to our cages.

Peter Meinke:
TO A DAUGHTER WITH ARTISTIC TALENT
—for Deijan Peri

I know why, getting up in the cold dawn
you paint cold yellow houses
and silver trees. Look at those green birds,

almost real, and that lonely child looking
at those houses and trees.
You paint (the best way) without reasoning,
to see what you feel, and green birds
are what a child sees.

Some gifts are not given: you
are delivered to them,
bound by chains of nerves and genes
stronger than iron or steel, although
unseen. You have painted every day
for as long as I can remember
and will be painting still
when you read this, some cold
and distant December when the child
is old and the trees no longer silver
but black fingers scratching a grey sky.

And you never know why (I was lying
before when I said I knew).
You never know the force that drives you wild
to paint that sky, that bird flying,
and is never satisfied today
but maybe tomorrow
when the sky is a surreal sea
in which you drown . . .

I tell you this with love and pride
and sorrow, my artist child
(while the birds change from green to blue to brown).

Linda Pastan:
APRIL

The young cherry trees
stick out their limbs
as awkwardly as foals
standing for the first time.
Around them the maples
are itchy with new growth,
and dogwoods stand
in ballet poses.
How many leaves
open their green shutters now
to let April through.

Philip Booth:
A LATE SPRING: EASTPORT

On the far side
of the storm
window, as close

as a tree
might grow to
a house,

beads of rain
hang cold
on the lilac:

at the tip of
each twig each
bud swells green;

tonight out
there each
branch will be

glazed, each
drop will
freeze solid:

the ice, at
sunrise, will
magnify every

single
bud; by this
time next

week, in-
side this
old glass,

the whole
room will
bloom.

Richard Snyder:
CHICAGO, SUMMER PAST

It is summer, city summer.
It is nineteen-thirty-or-forty-what?
Barney Ross is champ; we could figure it
from that, or perhaps from looking
back to skinny, teenage boys who lived south
of Wino West Madison on Halsted
and Sangamon and who swaggered up
Roosevelt Road kneading sponge rubber balls
from Woolworth's.
               Hot afternoons in dark-wombed
Glickman's, when a lull came to the
silver screen, there was a chorus of sweaty
squish. The young boxers' muscles are slow-born.
But forty-four hundred west the
girls are coming from their Hebrew lessons:
black-olive eyes, pimento lips; all
olive, ripe, and aware of it.
The boys clench and cramp their fingers and feel
a soft, inward squeeze like a rubber ball.

      "Chicago, Summer Past" is a memory poem from the far
days of my boyhood when we all emulated the boxer Barney
Ross by squeezing sponge rubber balls to strengthen muscles.
No boxers came from my neighborhood, but a couple of pool
sharks did. And we all clenched before the beauty of the westside girls.   —R.S.

25

Robert Currie:
BROTHERS

Yarrow had to learn it but he loved Young Jacob
the way he'd tug a finger with chubby hands
but not the way he'd scream at sudden noises
At Easter time Yarrow held the baby chick
rubbed the down on Jacob's cheek
When the beak closed upon his ear
got the howling stopped
Bruda Jacob said when he could talk
tumbling from his crib
and Yarrow swung him at the ceiling
taught him not to cry

In summer Yarrow took him through the fence
going farther every day
until they discovered berries
vivid in the brambles
With the first snow Young Jacob
stayed inside/eyes
as big as windows
until Yarrow showed him
how to roll the scary white
into a round and jolly man
who puffed upon a carrot

And it was Yarrow wore him out
with exploration of the pasture
brought him home the shortest way
past the hen house   the chopping block
just as Mother swung the axe
the chicken heaving back
from its severed head
whirling a crimson sphere

26

about their deadened feet
until its blood spilled on their boots
the circle of Young Jacob's cries
tightening like a noose

Gregory Orr:
GATHERING THE BONES TOGETHER
—*for Peter Orr*

When all the rooms of the house
fill with smoke, it's not enough
to say an angel is sleeping on the chimney.

ONE

A Night in the Barn

The deer carcass hangs from a rafter.
Wrapped in blankets, a boy keeps watch
from a pile of loose hay. Then he sleeps

and dreams about a death that is coming:
Inside him, there are small bones
scattered in a field
among burdocks and dead grass.
He will spend his life walking there,
gathering the bones together.

Pigeons rustle in the eaves.
At his feet, the German shepherd
snaps its jaws in its sleep.

TWO

A father and his four sons
run down a slope toward
a deer they just killed.
The father and two sons carry
rifles. They laugh, jostle,
and chatter together.
A gun goes off,
and the youngest brother
falls to the ground.
A boy with a rifle
stands beside him, screaming.

THREE

I crouch in the corner of my room,
staring into the glass well
of my hands; far down
I see him drowning in air.

Outside, leaves shaped like mouths
make a black pool
under a tree. Snails glide
there, little death-swans.

FOUR

Smoke

Something has covered the chimney
and the whole house fills with smoke.
I go outside and look up at the roof,
but I can't see anything.

I go back inside. Everyone weeps,
walking from room to room.
Their eyes ache. This smoke
turns people into shadows.
Even after it is gone, and the tears are gone,
we will smell it in pillows
when we lie down to sleep.

FIVE

He lives in a house of black glass.
Sometimes I visit him, and we talk.
My father says he is dead,
but what does that mean?
Last night I found a child
sleeping on a nest of bones.
He had a red, leaf-shaped
scar on his cheek. I lifted him up
and carried him with me, even though
I didn't know where I was going.

SIX

The Journey

Each night, I knelt on a marble slab
and scrubbed at the blood.
I scrubbed for years and still it was there.
But tonight the bones in my feet
begin to burn. I stand up
and start walking, and the slab
appears under my feet with each step,
a white road only as long as your body.

SEVEN

The Distance

The winter I was eight, a horse
slipped on the ice, breaking its leg.
Father took a rifle, a can of gasoline.
I stood by the road at dusk and watched
the carcass burning in the far pasture.

I was twelve when I killed him;
I felt my own bones wrench from my body.
Now I am twenty-seven and walk
beside this river, looking for them.
They have become a bridge
that arches toward the other shore.

꼿 This seven part poem was written as a way of coming to terms with personal anguish. It comes out of an incident in my life—my brother's death in a hunting accident for which I was responsible when I was twelve years old. We seem, as people, unable to talk about the events that most deeply affect our lives. I think poetry can do that, that's one of the reasons it's important. In the case of this poem, it's a story of sudden death, guilt, a sense of how fragile life is, how mysterious death is, and how persistent the effects of tragedy are. The worst thing about tragedy is that it isolates the people it affects. But by expressing feelings and describing experiences, a poem can make other people feel and thus break down two kinds of isolation: that isolation between two people and that deeper, more terrible isolation that cuts a person off from his own feeling self.

I'm a lyric poet—my subject is primarily feelings. In order to make them as intense as I feel them, I sometimes make them like dreams—I don't mean the phony, misty dreams out of old movies, but the precise, vivid ones we all have sometimes—we don't know exactly what they mean, but we *feel* they mean something, even if we can't translate it into ordinary conversation. A poem is one of those places where you can write about things that you know and feel are true without worrying about whether they are "real" in the ordinary sense. Poems can represent what another poet calls "heart-truths"—feelings and experiences out of our deepest selves.   —G.O.

Peter Wild:
ICE CREAM

Still unable to pronounce the months
I saw it come closer each week,
more real than the war.

once, stopping to throw rocks at the cows,
                    we rode out on our bicycles
past the trucks, each with its cloud,
the closest I'd come
          to a traveling circus.

my brother said they
were German prisoners
who waved back gleaming in their sweat,
so I yelled "Aufschnitt,"
then sped down the new road smooth as glass.

but woke to it next morning
gliding like lava making
its own path through our woods.

that night my father took us out
in the missing Buick.
            "Look, no hands!" he said
as our mother scowled,
        the Holsteins loomed in their pastures,
and we arrived in town
to drive back in one night.

but first circled up the mountain
to see the spot where years ago
he saw the Gypsies camped,
            dancing around their wagons,
as she scowled again and I
        took a bite of ice cream
    that drove a spike through my head.

Don Welch:
WE USED TO PLAY

a game called kick the can, which used to last about a month.
    That's how long it took to catch Fred Tooley.

Tooley was a fat kid. He used to pick his nose just after
    recess as if he hadn't purged himself enough in soccer.
    When the early fall would come in through the window,
    cold as a spoon against our cheeks, Tooley would sit
    in Math IV eating dirt stewed with asthma.

Miss Johnson said his system was lacking (this was always
    after she'd spanked his hands), but his brain wasn't.
    Tooley never hid more than 50 yards from the can in
    front of Harold's house, and we still spent months
    trying to find him. I'll never understand how he got

under the latticed facade of Bonehead Eiler's porch
one time. We found him with Bonehead's dog and 13
pups. He went to hide before she was bred.

As I said, it was just a game, but taken seriously enough
to take to bed. I remember how often I dreamed of
finding Tooley under a pile of leaves in the front
yard, or behind the seat of old man Arnold's tank
truck. I never dreamed of Tooley home in bed.

And I remember walking to school past Jim Hink's house
and wondering if Hink's father had eaten Fred. Old
man Hink was mean. There was this trail across the
backyard where he dragged dead spirit in his foot.
I remember the two lines of dirt and the thin line
of grass which old Hink's insole never touched. He
must have fit his foot to the ruts and ridden bearings
of dirt all the way to the back door. I guess that
was the only place in the neighborhood too narrow
for Fred Tooley.

But when I got to school there he'd be, leaning his fat
against those heavy doors we had to help the kinder-
garteners with. There he'd be, playing the aardvark,
sticking his tongue out, eating those soft beebees
for breakfast, and he'd say, "Wanna play kick the can?"

Paul Zimmer:
ZIMMER AND HIS TURTLE SINK THE HOUSE

I had soaked the old house
Until the plaster bulged like fungus
From its lath. Bead ferns grew

33

In the rainbow spray of
The waterfalls down the carpeted stairs,
And the meter in the cellar
Clicked off the waters of my mistake.

I had forgotten, gone away and left
My turtle burping through the water
Running in the upstairs sink,
Gone away and left the old house
Torpedoed and filling, with only
A cold-blooded helmsman on the bridge.

All the towels, old underwear and mops
That I could muster never dried
The house up, never turned
The meter back from what it told.

The turtle was gone.
Swept to the basement no doubt
Where he had grown into a loggerhead,
Grumbling and steel-jawed like my father,
Angry at my carelessness, ready to snap
My digits off if I gave him
Half a chance.

Donald Hall:
THE SLEEPING GIANT

a hill in Hamden, Connecticut

The whole day long, under the walking sun
That poised an eye on me from its high floor,
Holding my toy beside the clapboard house
I looked for him, the summer I was four.

34

I was afraid the waking arm would break
From the loose earth and rub against his eyes
A fist of trees, and the whole country tremble
In the exultant labor of his rise;

Then he with giant steps in the small streets
Would stagger, cutting off the sky, to seize
The roofs from house and home because we had
Covered his shape with dirt and planted trees;

And then kneel down and rip with fingernails
A trench to pour the enemy Atlantic
Into our basin, and the water rush,
With the streets full and all the voices frantic.

That was the summer I expected him.
Later the high and watchful sun instead
Walked low behind the house, and school began,
And winter pulled a sheet over his head.

Doug Cockrell:
FIST FIGHT

An uncontrollable night
and Mike wants more than blood,
wants the game of it—
more than his fists mushing up
Jimmy's face, this
athlete wants the crowd first
with hot dogs, beer, pop corn

as he takes Jimmy out
under the stars
in the once wild, impenetrable darkness
of the summer woods.

With unleashed fists
Mike and Jimmy whirl
in the headlight beams;
the dust makes the two ghosts
which finally materialize
with Jimmy falling like a human shadow
below Mike's stance in the light.

Mike keeps calling Jimmy back up;
disturbed birds
shake off their limbs
and fly deeper into the night . . .

Cheers come out of the ring of cars,
the winners tell the losers who they are:

celebration, music, the snap of beer cans
are amplified by the silence
around the loser's vehicles—buddies
who resign from that night's flourish

with apologetic condolences to Jimmy
who staggers punch drunk away from the ring.

Meanwhile, the winners drink on for Mike;
the city is outflanked upon the river.
Around the bonfires, motorcycles appear;
women blush up to the light
and not even a cop car goes by . . .

⌒ "Fist Fight" is based on certain truths: there was a fight
that summer night and Mike and Jimmy were the ones en-
gaged in the fighting. The fight occurred in the summer of 1971
and those two teenagers are now dead. Both had alcohol-re-
lated deaths in their mid-twenties. So the fight is significant
because of the limited amount of time the two had to build up
experience. This was an important fight in their lives.

Mike was an athlete in school and Jimmy was a cut-up. The
poem succeeds for the reason that the persona of the narrator
feels for the underdog, Jimmy, but still stands in awe of what
power Mike and his friends could unleash on a hot, summer
night.

Both fighters were popular and hence the drama of the scene.
The lines:

as he takes Jimmy out
under the stars

. . . evoke a primordial, mature quality which Mike and his
friends possessed as the dominant males in the tamed land
around Redfield, S.D.

The lines:

Cheers come out of the ring of cars,
the winners tell the losers who they are:

describe on one hand the triumph of Mike and his friends and
on the other hand the humiliation of Jimmy and his friends.

For two peer groups fought that night with their idols as the combatants. A little savagery reported here about the night life of teenagers in the Midwest. High tension was the result when these two groups met. The fight I imagine met the same epitome of excitement as a street fight would in the East.

For Mike, the night was his. The lines:

Meanwhile, the winners drink on for Mike;
the city is outflanked upon the river.
Around the bonfires, motorcycles appear;
women blush up to the light
and not even a cop car goes by . . .

demonstrate the possibility of lawlessness or freedom (whatever is your viewpoint) left in this country. The total victory of that night, contrasted to the total defeat of another, is real in the poem, therefore I feel successful. I had to write this poem because I felt that it was a meaningful (I'm not saying good) event in life. I know; I was there. I hope that the poem puts the reader there. If it does, then that makes the poem successful, too!   —D.C.

Gary Gildner:
FIRST PRACTICE

After the doctor checked to see
we weren't ruptured,
the man with the short cigar took us
under the grade school,
where we went in case of attack
or storm, and said
he was Clifford Hill, he was
a man who believed dogs
ate dogs, he had once killed

for his country, and if
there were any girls present
for them to leave now.
                        No one
left. OK, he said, he said I take
that to mean you are hungry
men who hate to lose as much
as I do. OK. Then
he made two lines of us
facing each other,
and across the way, he said,
is the man you hate most
in the world,
and if we are to win
that title I want to see how.
But I don't want to see
any marks when you're dressed,
he said. He said, *Now*.

∝ The school I attended when I was a boy was brand new, a parochial school, grades one through eight. We had few activities outside of classes and these were inevitably connected to the church—choir, setting up tables in the basement for Bingo, the perennial Paper Drive. We had no gym, no formal athletics. Our games were pickup games of softball and soccer at recess—and a particularly mad sport that we called, as I remember, "Pile-On." Someone would grab the soccer ball and run and everyone else would give chase and tackle him—*en masse*. The heady object, I think, was to possess the ball as long as possible.

One day our pastor, Father Gauthier, decided that we ought to be more organized, become more like the other Catholic schools in the city. He decided that we ought to field a football team. There was a league we could join consisting of teams manned by boys in the eighth grade; it was called the Knights of Columbus League and there was a big trophy at stake.

So on a fine Sunday morning Father Gauthier called from the pulpit for a coach. A former Marine, who had apparently played Service ball, responded. His name was Clifford, he was short and stocky, and he sucked a short cigar.

Now I should explain here that underneath our new school was a thick-walled basement with a low ceiling that was called The Bomb Shelter. There were no windows and the doors were of heavy metal. We all understood, when reminded, that that was where we must go if the Russians attacked. Meantime we used The Bomb Shelter during tornado warnings and bad storms; and it was an adventure to collect down there, following the nuns scurrying in their skirts, rosary beads clicking at their legs.

This period of which I speak—the 1950s—when ordinary citizens were known to bury bunkers in their back yards and victual them—did not truly make the frightened, crazy aspect of its character known to us, or at least to me, until later. I remember the summer that Bob Pillow and I answered a newspaper ad for construction work. We were in high school then, wanting to get in shape for football in the fall. Our employer—for one day—turned out to be a Minister of God (that's what he told us) who sold home bomb shelters on the side. He needed strong young men like ourselves, he said, to dig the holes. What we would have helped this man plant in the Michigan earth, we soon saw, were nothing more than giant tin cans fit perhaps for stewed meats. We were taking on knowledge.

But in the eighth grade The Bomb Shelter of our school was another matter; it was another matter entirely when—after a doctor listened to our hearts and felt under our shorts and told us to cough—Cliff ushered us in there and closed the heavy metal door.

My best friend in the eighth grade was Pat Arsenault. We

were just about the same size. He was the one who stood across from me in Cliff's design to slug away at and be slugged at in return—but not in the face, where outsiders might read what the Holy Redeemer boys had been up to.

Some of us later felt slimy and ashamed at hitting out like that—at being *moved* by Cliff's speech. And I know that many of us were more afraid to lose a game than to break a bone. But we all felt proud when, at the conclusion of that successful season, Father Gauthier took the team to Frankenmuth, famous for its chicken dinners, and treated us to a big feed, including all the ice cream we could eat, and the gleaming trophy we deserved.

For years I tried to write a short story about this experience, but the attempts always sounded wrong, false. One day I decided to simply "list" the story's important elements. Except for one unnecessary word, the poem "First Practice" appeared.

—G.G.

Gregory Orr:
ADOLESCENCE

The dog barks from a cloud
after each car passes
and a fine powder settles
on yard shrubs. In late spring
the county truck sprays
oil on the road, binding
the dust. I strip
catkins from willows
and beat the air
with insane intensity.
Reeds bending in wind;
electrical hum
from a roadside pole.
Behind the red house, gray
clouds and the rumble
of summer thunder. Above,
yellow, spiked globes swell
among the deep green
chestnut leaves. And in the hay,
can't breathe; can't
breathe in the hay. Hands
on skin; how good it feels.

Jonathan Holden:
AN AMERICAN BOYHOOD

There was little important
to do but chew gum, or count
the ways a flipped jack-knife
caught in the dirt.
One Sunday afternoon I had an idea.

We clamped the cables of Tommy
Emory's train transformer
to a steel pie plate
filled with salt water
and drank through our fingers
the current's purr,
dialing that bird-heartbeat
higher, riding its flutter until
both hands were bucked
out of water.
                 We knew
we were wasting our time,
though we had nothing
but time. Our parents
moved vague among their great
worries, remote
as the imperatives of weather.
And the stars appeared on schedule
to run their dim, high errands
again, leaving us lost
in the long boredom of our childhood,
flipping our knives in the dust,
waiting to find out just how
in this world we were going
to be necessary.

◎ It was a Sunday afternoon in autumn, and a gang of
neighborhood boys, all around eleven or twelve years old, had
gathered across the street on Everts' steps. They had nothing
they wanted to do and were aimlessly exchanging insults, practicing how to spit, pushing each other, fencing with scraps of
molding. They were almost beside themselves with boredom
and wouldn't have minded getting into trouble—anything to
spice up that Sunday.

I was trying to read, but I was conscious of their presence

outdoors—a nervous force that could explode. Then I put down my book. It had come to me with the clarity of revelation how much my own boyhood had been spent like that, with nothing to do, trying to ward off boredom by means of some useless activity—skimming stones, shooting baskets, flipping a jack-knife, or just trying to look tough. Everybody else around us—adults, birds, even the weather—had seemed to have a job; but for us there had been nothing to do but kill time. I realized that even as a boy I had felt humiliated by my own idleness—I had been chagrined by it—and that, just like these boys at Everts', I'd tried to cover that up by acting tough or by hanging out with other kids in order to appear occupied.

I went immediately upstairs to my desk and started the poem. As I searched for memories of the kinds of things we used to do to kill time, I remembered rigging up the pie-plate with an older kid named Grant Howell. Somehow that activity—in its pure uselessness and its unlikely ingenuity—typified the lengths we'd go to in order to find something with which to amuse ourselves. Most of my poem consists of story-telling, but the ending attempts to do something which, in poetry, may be the most difficult feat: I try to make a plain statement. The ending hints at the deep anxiety that lurked just beneath my boyhood boredom—the suspicion that my very being might not be necessary or wanted in this world at all.

This poem, like all of my poems, tries to clarify my feelings about some part of my experience. I believe that is the purpose of a poem—to give shape, in a concise and memorable way, to what our lives feel like. In this way, poems help us to notice the world more and better, and they enable us to share with others, who may still be looking for the right words, the words we have found, through art, to express many of the deepest and subtlest aspects of our experience.   —J.H.

David Allan Evans:
BULLFROGS
—*for Ernie, Larry, and Bob*

sipping a Schlitz
we cut off the legs,
packed them in ice, then
shucked the rest back into
the pond for turtles

ready to go home
we looked down and saw
what we had thrown back in:
quiet-bulging eyes nudging along
the moss's edge, looking up at us,

asking for their legs

☙ I can watch bullfrogs for hours. They "sit" in muck
(imagine their lean, miler's legs, which you can't see, dangling
in the water) waiting . . . waiting for anything that moves.
Whatever is motionless doesn't interest them. Down through
the slimy eons they have been programmed only for things
flying or crawling. Put something on a hook (worm, a piece of
cloth), or just use the bare hook itself and cast it beyond them
and then reel it in, dragging it close enough for them to see it,
and watch what happens. Immediately they turn—if not already turned toward it—and face it. If the object stops, they
suddenly forget it. If it moves again, they lurch at it, sometimes
squeaking. Gulp! They have it, and look as if nothing has happened. They go about their business of sitting in the muck,
waiting . . .

So my friends and I, almost every summer when the muck
was thick and green enough (you can't get them in open

water—they go sleek like a fish and keep disappearing), went after them with fishing rods.

My poem came directly out of the experience. I don't know if we were actually drinking Schlitz beer, but I like the slurpy, amphibious sound of that word in the first line, along with "sipping." I wanted to present the scene very objectively, almost as a scientist, so I was a little surprised when I came to the end of the poem in which the dead (not *too* dead!) frogs-without-legs kept "looking up at us" and then, as it seemed, began, without words, not begging but:

asking for their legs

That's what they looked like they were doing. I admit the poem has some guilt in it, though it's not obvious. The fact *behind* the poem is that the experience described here was the *first* time we de-legged the frogs, and we didn't know they would survive, even for hours, after the de-legging. I need to quickly add that, from then on we made sure they were dead—stone dead—before we took their legs for a meal.

That eerie image of the frogs with their "quiet-bulging eyes nudging along the moss's edge, looking up at us" is still in my head. It's that image that got the poem going. The last line, as I remember, just said itself to me. What it said is the same thing another poet said centuries ago:

The boys kill frogs for sport,
but the frogs die in earnest.   —D.A.E.

Keith Wilson:
THE LAMB

carved in cheap marble, milky & veined
rests unengraved, a gesture without
other sign on a small grave of my childhood.

the wind blew, &
having blown

flecked the surface, leveled the heaped
earth. On the high hill overlooking
the small village of my childhood a
lamb lay guarding the changing dust,
the years that raced by my hunting

—carrying a .22, out walking the mesas
by & beyond the Hill, it was the Lamb
I went to, amazed at the changing
stone

the marker, looking always East,
shrinking as the dusty wind blew
the knived sand, blew always
from the North, high hill country
where stranger animals than the
rabbits I hunted growled & stirred
in the wind that ate the stone away
I walked, my face roughening in the cold.

David McElroy:
BEFORE BREAKUP ON THE CHENA OUTSIDE
FAIRBANKS

We flung gravel out in arcs then cut
for trees. Now shattered water answers
back. We laugh, and your hair is tender.
I cup it in my hands. Cars attack the bridge,
headlights splash, and your brown skin goes cream.

That light makes tall dogs impractical now,
bisects children, and crossing the bridge,
cuts an edge where runny noses wobble.
Last spring your dad clawed for air when ice broke
under runners and half-breed team. Ling cod sucked

his clothes. Babies are jelly now in the walls of rabbits
and that river's wall. I think this bent fender
is Ford. That ankle, hair, hock and antler you know.
Your face is native in my hands. Owl feathers catch
in a white wall tire I can't explain. All rivers

have tires. Across the Chena a husky bitch bangs
a chain anchored in her throat. In a minute
you'll sing or cry again and rub your knees.
Look, you say, the snow when you walk on it
is like a leather wallet when you twist it.

Here a fox pinned a meal beneath his weight.
We kiss here, and our story is tracked in snow.
The way we came, running the razor water and gravel
and there your frigid angel where I explained
the blood each month and blood the first time.

∝ I came to write the poem "Before Breakup on the Chena
Outside Fairbanks" a year or so after taking a walk with a girl
one night in early spring along the Chena River. The incident
stayed with me, working on my memory and imagination (the
two fuse together somehow) until I found myself trying to make
a poem that expressed a feeling I had about the incident. The
poem is not a narrative of that walk, the real one, but I'm
wanting you to think it is. Some things from real life seemed
important to keep as they were, to say or imply they were. We
did run around and throw gravel that broke the tinselly ice

that had formed with darkness on the new melt. She was native, Athabaskan. Her father had drowned the year before while crossing bad ice. We did see junk. She cried thinking of rivers and her father. I felt sorry for her, for the dirty harshness of the world in which living things are so vulnerable, for myself, even, a part of that dirty harshness and vulnerability.

But I also felt this mixture of crazy, horney, raciness along with the sorrow. Most of our feelings are perhaps some amalgamation of such inharmonious elements, I think. Anyway, the only way I could express them was in the poem itself. I did not want a nice poem. I did not want a nice white boy oozing with sympathy for an innocent sorrowing Indian maiden under the northern lights. Any of us are too complex for that kind of type-casting. I wanted the poem to not answer anything. I wanted it to sort of kick the reader in the face just a little at the end. After trying to assume the teacher role of explainer, I want the reader to question my motives. And if, as I think happens, the reader tends to identify with the narrator of the poem, even if just for a few moments, then he or she too will feel a little buzz of recognition of self awareness. If this were a sketch, it would be heavy jagged lines around the curve of hair and fender, hands and the arcing spray of gravel stopped in headlights.   —D.McE.

Don Welch:
SPADE SCHARNWEBER

Spade Scharnweber was a white Watusi. His mother,
  who was an even 5 feet, had nightmares of giving
  birth to a foreigner who never stopped unspooling.

And Spade laid two claims to fame.

49

One, he had to have an extended rod welded to his bike
seat so that when he rode he could keep his knees
out of his salivaries.

But the other was more renown. Spade was the only
letterman who was tall enough to lie across the
ceiling panels from the boys' locker room to where
the girls were dressing.

We held his feet as if they were a witching wand, and
when Spade trembled, we knew his eyes were there.

When his arches inflated, we knew he'd seen Ina Claire
Frischoltz, and for a poor equivalent, he once
showed us one of those girlie cards Eagles used
to carry from their Aerie.

But by the time he was a senior, I guess his mother's
turnips had done their thing. His clavicles
thickened, and his bones grew so heavy they spoke
loads of sand. So we shouldn't have been surprised
when Spade fell through the ceiling tiles one day
and hung like a limp joint over studs that held
two laughing, screaming walls.

As we held his milk-of-magnesia ankles, Miss Charlotte
Crue, PE teacher and civics coach, slapped his
face with a virginal towel 7 adolescent light years
from his toes.

And Ina Claire tells me the hole's still there, that
Stockville girls still expect a mantis in a maroon
letter sweater to descend upon them with bug eyes,
somehow thickening their grace.

తా "Spade Scharnweber" is the result of two real-life experiences. The first, which happened to one of my daughters, occurred when she was showering with some other junior high girls. A fat boy plunged through the ceiling panels of the girls' locker room and landed at her feet. The girls scattered, and the boy, embarrassed, more or less dribbled over into a corner where he hunkered down with his hands over his face.

The other was my close high school friendship with a boy named Merritt Scharnweber. When we were sophomores, the coach measured us for the basketball program. Scharnweber, a human splinter, was 6′ 5″ and weighed 135 lbs. I wasn't much better, weighing in at 130, just under 6′ tall. But Scharnweber had an astounding metabolic growth. While I remained skinny, as a senior he shot up to over 6′ 6″ and 225 lbs. This height and weight made him the right character for this poem.

Of course, no athletic hero goes around with a name like Merritt. So I used his nickname, which was given to him one day by an all-state end named Nickolite. Looking down at Scharnweber's feet, this end asked him what size shoes he wore, and when Scharnweber answered, "15 E," Nickolite, who was all man (or so he thought) and never intentionally spoke a simile, exclaimed, "Your feet are like spades!" From that time on, Scharnweber, known as Spade, had a name appropriate to his stature.

But there is a time when high school boys, believing their superiority in athletics carries over to life itself, become especially ripe for a fall. Something in the universe always takes care of over-reachers, and in the poem Scharnweber gets it right in the kisser, via a towel in the hands of tiny Charlotte Crue, an old, but feisty teacher.

I like this poem because it tells a story people apparently like. I remember the fun I had in writing it, even laughing out loud when I discovered what I thought was the right exaggerated word or phrase. If readers like it well enough to go back a second time, I would like them to listen especially to its sounds and rhythms. Although it looks like prose, it isn't. Too many sounds and rhythms repeat themselves too fre- quently. —D.W.

William Matthews:
IN MEMORY OF THE UTAH STARS

Each of them must have terrified
his parents by being so big, obsessive
and exact so young, already gone
and leaving, like a big tipper,
that huge changeling's body in his place.
The prince of bone spurs and bad knees.

The year I first saw them play
Malone was a high school freshman,
already too big for any bed,
14, a natural resource.
You have to learn not to
apologize, a form of vanity.
You flare up in the lane, exotic
anywhere else. You roll the ball
off fingers twice as long as your
girlfriend's. Great touch for a big man,
says some jerk. Now they're defunct
and Moses Malone, boy wonder at 19,
rises at 20 from the St. Louis bench,
his pet of a body grown sullen
as fast as it grew up.

Something in you remembers every
time the ball left your fingertips
wrong and nothing the ball

can do in the air will change that.
You watch it set, stupid moon,
the way you watch yourself
in a recurring dream.
You never lose your touch
or forget how taxed bodies
go at the same pace they owe,
how brutally well the universe
works to be beautiful,
how we metabolize loss
as fast as we have to.

⧆ Like many Americans, I'm fascinated by sports. There's little record in our literature, however, what this fascination means to us. On some level it's like TV and junk food; on some other level, though, it enlivens deep and powerful emotions in us. "In Memory of the Utah Stars" is a poem I wrote to investigate and make more explicit some of those emotions.

The Utah Stars were a member team in the old American Basketball Association. Late in its last season the team was disbanded—the ownership couldn't meet a payroll. Suddenly the gifted and special young men who were the players were without security and adulation they had come to take for granted.

I think sports are about time, change and loss, and about striving to be special while learning to bear the unavoidable freight of disappointment and ordinariness. That also seems to me a good description of growing up.

Moses Malone, the boy hero of the poem, has gone on since I wrote it to become one of the greatest basketball players of all time. Sports are also about the sweet ferocity of excellence. For most of us, the task of the other ex-Stars is closer to our own: not to see time as a series of lost, receding Edens, but to live as fully as we can whatever possibilities are ours, moment to moment. But even Moses's task is exemplary, and the sulking and terrified boy who appears in my poem is an earlier but not a different Moses Malone from the one we now know of, disappeared as he may seem to be into his camouflage of mastery. —W.M.

Jonathan Holden:
SEVENTEEN

That June before the judge gave
Rennie Dodd his choice—jail or joining
the Marines—we were already on patrol, part
of the nervous prod of traffic
along the cement tundra called U.S. 46,
observing protocol. Drunk,
swerving at oncoming cars, giving
pedestrians the finger,
we'd rake the AM tuner's roar
for bursts of action at the front, chasing
that low blaze on the horizon.
But this was 1959. There was no war.
We were invited
nowhere. We had to cross the state line
to buy beer. Our tires peeling their awkward
falsetto, we'd head out on a mission, sure
that, this time, the skyline was inviting
us, and eager to go, ready
to be recruited by the night.

X. J. Kennedy:
AT A LOW MASS FOR TWO HOT-RODDERS

Sheeted in steel, embedded face to face,
They idle in a feelingless embrace,
The only ones at last who had the nerve
To crash head-on, not chicken out and swerve.
Inseparable, in one closed car they roll
Down the stoned aisle and on out to a hole,
Wheeled by the losers; six now shorn of beard,

Black-jacketed and glum, who also steered
Toward absolute success with total pride,
But, inches from it, felt, and turned aside.

Phil Hey:
THE TRUE BALLAD OF THE GREAT RACE TO GILMORE CITY

Big Ralph from Rolfe had a black Corvette
The fastest one you ever met
A 454, dual AFB's
That car had power like a dog has fleas
A set of Hijackers all around
A couple of Thrushes for that low-down sound
Four Cragar mags and Mickeys on the back
A terror on the street or on the track was Big Ralph
                                         from Rolfe

Now Ralph made it known far and wide
He had no equals for that Corvette ride
On his slower days just to pass the time
He'd beat a bunch of Smokeys to the county line
All the cars he raced he left in the dust
So far back they couldn't hear his exhaust
Ralph thought that car was the very last word
But you can bet he never heard of Peggy
                                   from Poky

Peggy had a Trans-Am 455
That just for starters ate hemis alive
Dual quads, hot cam and a bored-out block
But outside it looked just plain stock
Sweet innocence in baby blue
Til she fired it up and then you knew

That Firebird could go like a jet
An easy match for the black Corvette of Big Ralph
from Rolfe

They set up a meeting one moonlit night
Highway Three was the racing site
From the junction of Fifteen to Gilmore City
Let it all hang out and take no pity
The bet was on and the word spread far
The loser was going to give up the car
They lined the road for miles to see
If Ralph would win or if it would be Peggy
from Poky

The flag went down and the squeal and the roar
Made the earth shake all the way to Thor
With a ton of torque and a thousand-horse load
They left rubber on a mile of road
Now she had the traction but he had the speed
All the power they had was the power they'd need
Peggy thought she had an easy ride
Until she looked over and there beside her was Ralph
from Rolfe

Nose to nose and wheel to wheel
Came them screaming shapes of steel
She went into second at one-twenty-four
His tach read ten-five with room for more
With a hand like lightning he went into third
But he just couldn't leave that baby blue Bird
And through the thundering night they sped
With Gilmore City just a mile ahead for Peggy
from Poky

But before Ralph would let her beat him down
He'd run wide open through Gilmore Town

He put his foot through the firewall
And the Vette shot ahead winner take all
But after he passed the city line
Peggy caught up and gave him the sign
He tried to shut down but was going too fast
He wiped out the town and it looked like the last of Big Ralph
from Rolfe

When they saw the end of the smoke and the noise
That black Corvette looked like Tinkertoys
And Peggy was sure there was nothing to do
Until she heard a voice come through
Said, Listen honey, I'm all right
But I think I'll need a ride home tonight
She said, You don't need another word
Cause you just won a baby blue Bird from Peggy
from Poky

Well folks I think you know the rest
That Trans-Am soon became joint possessed
And Ralph and Peggy formed a racing team
The likes of which you ain't ever seen
You can talk about Daytona and them other races
You can talk about LeMans and them other places
You can talk about Indy til you're blue in the face
But there'll never be another like that great race between Ralph
and Peggy

√ Obviously, I don't have any great literary motives for this
ballad, nor any great literary hopes. I wrote it mostly for fun—
to entertain the kids at Rolfe High School and their great
teacher Betty Knoll—but then I had to ask myself what went
into it.

I grew up in the Fifties, the great age of cars and lowdown

songs about them, and I always liked the directness of people who like cars and car songs. Of course, when you're living through something, you never quite know what's going to matter later. What got to me most, and still does, is technical slang—the way people talk about the machines they like and use. And it always tickled me that friends who got D's in English could talk for hours on end about cars, using a sophisticated vocabulary that was completely foreign to their teachers. And then, I think that people relate to fast cars and drivers the same way they used to relate to knights in shining armor. You don't have to believe anything in a story of either knights or drivers to get involved in the flow of the story and the language that presents it. One more time, it's for fun, as a lot of poetry should be. If you have a literary interpretation, hmm, try to keep it to yourself (or write and surprise me).   —P.H.

Stanley Kunitz:
END OF SUMMER

An agitation of the air,
A perturbation of the light
Admonished me the unloved year
Would turn on its hinge that night.

I stood in the disenchanted field
Amid the stubble and the stones,
Amazed, while a small worm lisped to me
The song of my marrow-bones.

Blue poured into summer blue,
A hawk broke from his cloudless tower,
The roof of the silo blazed, and I knew
That part of my life was over.

Already the iron door of the north
Clangs open: birds, leaves, snows
Order their populations forth,
And a cruel wind blows.

Maxine Kumin:
THE MUMMIES

Two nights running I was out there
in orange moonlight with old bedsheets
and a stack of summered-over Sunday papers
tucking up the tomatoes while the peppers
whimpered and went under and the radishes
dug in with their dewclaws and all over
the field the goldenrod blackened
and fell down like Napoleon's army.

This morning they're still at it, my tomatoes
making marbles, making more of those little
green volunteers that you can rattle
all winter in a coat pocket, like fingers.
But today on the lip of the solstice
I will pull them, one hundred
big blind greenies. I will stand them
in white rows in the root cellar
wrapped one by one
in the terrible headlines.

Richard Wilbur:
EXEUNT

    Piecemeal the summer dies;
At the field's edge a daisy lives alone;
   A last shawl of burning lies
     On a gray field-stone.

    All cries are thin and terse;
The field has droned the summer's final mass;
   A cricket like a dwindled hearse
     Crawls from the dry grass.

Keith Wilson:
TWIN ACES

back to back, Stud poker & an open
pot. The play, intense, grew harder.
Clark, Bowers, McMorris & my dad, cool
professionals: "Poker's for men," my dad'd
say, paying out his debts with grocery money,
bringing his tales with flushed face to our
quiet home. Great stories from the tall
fierce combats he lived for

               while I, a comrade,
a spy posted by mother, sat by propping
my eyes open & pleasing father who thought
at last I'd shown a normal interest.

             Thick cigar smoke
& the sharp smell of whiskey, I remember
that, & the naked bulb, those men
flicking cards into the pot of light
slitted eyes watching their fall
as if it were their own:

                 yet my father won
with a slipped ace & we got out quick
before the discards were counted. Walking
home, 4 a.m., my father singing & looking
back over his shoulder, the quiet street
behind him.

Robert Currie:
JULY THE FIRST

1
Yarrow counted eight of them
young guys at the door
his father laughing like a kid
enjoying their proposal
   Sure he said sure thing
   I'll try and make a comeback
   but it's gotta be in the contract
   Yarrow goes along as batboy

2
In the box of Fulton's truck
they rode together telling stories
passing round and round
a jug of homemade wine
Yarrow embarrassed once
when they offered him a shot
Before they made the turn
to the Yellowgrass Reserve
someone remembered
and pitched the bottle out
Then they hit the dirt trail
bouncing over ruts and badger holes
to the diamond in the pasture

3
Yarrow watched puppets on a hayrack
bingo in a stained canvas tent
He bet a quarter on a horse-race
Indian ponies ridden bareback
galloped down a quarter-mile
Yarrow leaning through the finish line

helped his quarter multiply
Then he lay in uncut grass
with half a rhubarb pie inside
He studied miles of prairie sky
staring at a streaming cloud
that raced beyond the sun
his skin warm   alive
in blowing grass

4

His father played without a mask
jammed in tight behind the plate
one knee planted on the ground
caught well too   and hit
threw out a man at second
led his team into the money
the final game that lingered
through the creeping dusk

5

He'd never heard him scream before
his father falling from the foul
that split his thumb to bone
Yarrow rushed to hold him but
he pulled away   he strode away
blustered   laughed
    it's nothin I can still play
    Put a chaw of tobacco on it
    some tape to hold her there
    Let's get on with the game
The colour dying slowly on his face
In the seventh inning
just before the game
was called for darkness
he hit a home run
to win it all

6
Yarrow lay in the truck box
curled against his father's chest
with singing all around
He watched the sky the stars
a bright one in the west
pulsing like a heart

～I grew up in the city, but what I remember about growing up was the attraction of the countryside and especially of
Round Hill, which lay across the railway trestle, a mere half
mile south of town. There, we camped overnight, wallowing
in an exuberant freedom from school and adults, glorying in
that brief hiatus before age and responsibility took their toll,
while we ran almost naked in our private Eden, browned by
the slowly turning summer sun, chilled by the night sounds of
darkening woods and creek, wandering sometimes to the rolling prairie where we hunted gophers with bows and arrows,
or in spring swimming with every nerve alive in water that felt
as if it had thawed only hours before.

Many springs have come and gone since then, but the memories of boyhood are still fresh as ice upon the tongue and—I
suspect—at the root of much of what I write. I remember, for
example, a Dominion Day when I was twelve and the thrill of
being invited to accompany a ball team to a tournament on
the Yellow Grass Reserve. Though I chased balls, carried water
and bats, cheered until my throat was raw, our team lost the
final game, the one with all the money on it. Years later—
when I thought I'd forgotten all about that Sports Day—it came
back again, clear and precise, though altered too by memory
and desire. Then I wrote a poem about a boy, Yarrow, and his
father who did not lose the final game. Poetry, after all, obeys
its own rules.

This father and son obeyed their own rules too, refusing to
fade away when the poem was done. Instead, a family was

65

born around them, one poem leading inevitably to another as I tried to explore the farm and small-town world in which they lived. I was on to something worth doing, something I believed that I could do. It was Robert Frost who said, "You're always believing ahead of your evidence. What was the evidence I could write a poem? I just believed it. The most creative thing in us is to believe a thing in . . ." Well, I would believe a poem sequence in, poem after poem until a whole story was told.

It was like shucking off a strait jacket. I was no longer limited to what could be done in a single poem. Instead, poems could build on one another, play off one another, contradict one another, the tensions growing from poem to poem, themes resonating back and forth, truths emerging even in the silences between the poems. Here was a new freedom to create. And it was my family to create, my world they lived in—or it was until the family demanded its own life, arguing, loving, aging, inescapably torn by the conflicts that are an authentic part of any family's life.

Poetry, I've always felt, is a heightened response to life, experience closely observed, highly imagined, then touched somehow by an indefinable magic as it is preserved on paper. For Yarrow, the magic lay in the way he went on, riding the life within him, vaulting from poem to poem until I had a book. He was worth believing in.   —R.C.

Gary Gildner:
MY FATHER AFTER WORK

Putting out the candles
I think of my father asleep
on the floor beside the heat,
his work shoes side by side
on the step, his cap

capping his coat on a nail,
his socks slipping down,
and the gray hair over his ear
marked black by his pencil.

Putting out the candles
I think of winter, that quick
dark time before dinner
when he came upstairs after
shaking the furnace alive,
his cheek patched with soot,
his overalls flecked with
sawdust and snow,
and called for his pillow,
saying to wake him
when everything was ready.

Putting out the candles
I think of going away
and leaving him there,
his tanned face turning
white around the mouth,
his left hand under his head
hiding a blue nail,
the other slightly curled
at his hip, as if
the hammer had just
fallen out of it
and vanished.

David Allan Evans:
THE STORY OF LAVA

Every time I smell Lava soap it is 1948.
My father is bending over a long sink in the
pressroom of *The Sioux City Journal* at 5 A.M.,
his grey long-underwear peeled down over his
white belly, a thin bar of Lava tumbling over
and over slowly in his ink-stained hands.
The morning news has passed through his hands
out into the morning streets into the hands
of sleepy boys who fold it a certain way and
fling it on porches and steps, but that is not
my story. Lava is my story and the morning
news that Lava can't rub off. It is my father
bending over a sink, a thin bar of Lava tumbling
over and over and over slowly in his cloudy hands.

Roy Scheele:
THE GAP IN THE CEDAR
—in memory of my father

I saw this much from the window:
the branch spring lightened into place
with a lithe shudder of snow.

Whatever bird had been there,
chickadee or sparrow,
had so vanished into air,

resilient, beyond recall,
it had to be taken on faith
to be taken at all.

In the moment it took the tree
to recover that trembling
something went wide in me—

there was a rush of wings,
the air beaten dim with snow,
and then I saw through the swirling.

∽ On November 11, 1972, after a lengthy illness, my father died in a hospital bed as I sat in a waiting room down the corridor. A few minutes after I heard the news, I went to his room and saw him, peaceful now after several years of pain, and then I noticed something on the portable stand beside the bed. It was a small sheet of notepaper, and on it was scrawled, in his unmistakable hand, "I don't understand everything that's happened . . ."

Neither did I. I had been very close to my father—when I was growing up, playing football and baseball, he was often in the stands to cheer me on, and in later years I would talk to him for hours about things that were on my mind, or be regaled by one of his many stories—and I wanted very much, after the first shock of his loss had subsided, to write an elegy for him.

Nine days after he died I wrote the following poem:

The glimmer of thought in those eyes,
their glint of humor,
and what was rarest, best, about them,
their glancing blue

it comes back to me now
in the snowflake that settles
like a wayward wreath
in the cedar.

Father, that look of yours,
always particular,
held true to the end . . .

The wet cedar branch is blue.

Almost immediately I was dissatisfied with the poem; while it did pick out a notable feature which might be taken as representative of my father's character, it fell far short of all I felt.

It snowed again one morning shortly afterwards, and that afternoon I passed by the front window just in time to see, with almost the clarity of a vision, one trembling branch of the cedar send down a thin shower of snow in the half-light. I had seen a sparrow in the tree earlier that day, and I assumed that it (or some other bird) had shaken down the snow in taking off from the branch. The happenstance of my witnessing this little natural event had provided me with a physical image of my father's death, something like seeing the flight of his soul, and I felt a curious and powerful elation that lasted for days.

All of this bided its time somewhere deep inside me. On the morning of January 5, 1973, hearing the words as if they were being spoken to me, I wrote the first three stanzas of the poem as they stand now, making only one minor change as I went, and a fourth stanza which I cancelled two days later when I returned to the poem, substituting the present fourth stanza and adding a fifth.

It is an unusual elegy—the person elegized is not even mentioned in the text of the poem—yet it is for precisely this reason that I feel the poem succeeds. It argues presence from absence, describing the natural event that reconciled me to my father's death. I like to think that in his shy way he would have approved of that.   —R.S.

Ralph Pomeroy:
BETWEEN HERE AND ILLINOIS

When my father died
I didn't get my brother's telegram.

Tuesday, the day my sister called,
I wasn't home.
It was sunny at the beach.

On Wednesday I got up at eight,
drank a glass of cold Tropicana,
had raisin toast, instant coffee,
went off to work.

That day my brother flew my father's body
from San Fernando to Illinois.

The rest of the week went by.
I was home all the following Sunday
because it was too cold to go swimming.

Monday, my sister reached me.
In the atmosphere of my office
I heard her voice, all the way from Michigan.

She said that the funeral was over.
She described the black vestments and white flowers.
She said that they had all missed me
and were wondering where I was.

If they had reached me
I could have flown from New York to Illinois—
all the way from here to Illinois—
over all the graves that lie between here and Illinois.

71

Doug Cockrell:
HIS LUNCH BUCKET

was the love between them
bottom dented out,
shaking as he walked
from the table at evening,

filled in his sleep
as it came and went with his cap;

most noons welcome
as mail between them
packed neatly with daily contents,
eaten whether on the move, in fields
or closed in shade of a barn, yet

when she forgot or just ran out,
he'd be whole days
hot as his thermos—
ready finally to
cuss into the bucket . . .

With all he left her then
to lay open

bitten.

Stanley Kunitz:
THE PORTRAIT

My mother never forgave my father
for killing himself,
especially at such an awkward time
and in a public park,
that spring
when I was waiting to be born.
She locked his name
in her deepest cabinet
and would not let him out,
though I could hear him thumping.
When I came down from the attic
with the pastel portrait in my hand
of a long-lipped stranger
with a brave moustache
and deep brown level eyes,
she ripped it into shreds
without a single word
and slapped me hard.
In my sixty-fourth year
I can feel my cheek
still burning.

⟨⟩ When I was a boy in Worcester, Massachusetts, I used to travel miles on my bike in order to go swimming in a lake outside the city limits that was known as Webster Lake. The reason I went there, in preference to more accessible bodies of water, was that I had discovered, while browsing through a local history at the public library, that the Indians long ago had given that lake a name, reputed to be the longest lake name in the world. I practiced how to say it and to this day still have it on my tongue. This is how it goes: Lake Chauggogagogmanchauggagogchabunagungamaugg . . . meaning I-fish-on-my-side you-fish-on-your-side nobody-fishes-in-the-middle. That knowledge gave me a secret power. I suppose it is in the nature of the poet, beginning in childhood, to love the sounds of language. Others may swim in Webster Lake, but poets swim in Lake Chauggogagogmanchauggagogchabuna-gungamaugg. And while others in my generation may have thought of redskins as howling savages, I knew from a single word that they believed in diplomacy and wanted to live peacefully with their neighbors.

A poem is at once the most primitive and the most sophisticated use of language. It has its roots in magic—in the spell over things delivered by the priest or shaman of the tribe. The words of a poem go back to the beginnings of the human adventure when the first syllables were not spoken but sung or chanted or danced. So it is that poetry always seems about to burst into song, to break into dance, but the secret of the poet's mastery is that he refrains from crossing over—the words stay words, they remain language.

Above all, poetry is intended for the ear. It must be felt to be understood, and before it can be felt it must be heard. Poets listen for their poems, and we, as readers, must listen in turn. If we listen hard enough, who knows?—we too may break into dance, perhaps for grief, perhaps for joy.

"Never try to explain," I say in the course of one of my poems, and that seems to me excellent advice to follow. When I read interpretations of my own work I am often puzzled by what others have found in it. A poem does not tell what it means, even to its maker. A prime source of its power is that it has its roots in the secrecy of a life and that it means more than it says. And a poem demands of its readers that they must come out to meet it, at least as far as it comes out to meet them, so that *their* meaning may be added to its. A common fallacy is to think that a poem begins with a meaning which then gets dressed up in words. On the contrary, a poem is language surprised in the act of changing into meaning.

One of my supreme influences was that visionary soul, William Blake, from whom I learned that generalization is the refuge of scoundrels and hypocrites, whereas art and science exist in the organization of Minute Particulars. Nearly all my poems are attached to a specific location and have their source in a definite experience.

The occasion of "End of Summer" is still vivid to me. I was living in the country, in Bucks County, Pennsylvania, and one day, at the turning of the season, while I was hoeing in the field, I heard a clamor in the sky and looked upward to see wave after wave of wild geese thundering south in their V-formations. In the actual process of writing, the geese flew out of the poem, but even now, when I read the lines aloud, I can hear the beating of their wings. As for "The Portrait," I have nothing left to say except that more years than I want to count have passed, according to the relentless calendar, since my widowed mother and I acted out our wordless drama in the house on Providence Street in Worcester; and it might as well be yesterday. Memory is each man's poet-in-residence. —S.K.

Gary Gildner:
POEMS

I sent my mother copies of my poems in print
to show her I was not a complete failure
and could do something besides
write dirty stories, and she was so happy

she replied with a poem of her own
about her heart waiting for spring and the beautiful
blue sky and some other lovelies
I don't remember, without calling it a poem

but you could tell that's what it was
because she lined it all out. The prettiest part
of her letter, however, was the end
where she said in her own true voice

"but mainly I can't wait for spring
because then my old man can get
to his garden and won't be bellyaching—
Oh he'll track in dirt and his hands

will never be clean and his breath
you can bet will be one big onion
once they get ripe, but it makes you
feel so good in your bones and it's all free!"

Hayden Carruth:
MENDING THE ADOBE

Sun dazzle and black shadow,
crow caw and magpie rattle
where I saw a pueblo woman,
dark and small, who stood
on a ponderosa block
outside her home to smear
rich mud on the wall, red
and oily mud, using her
hands and a thin wooden
paddle. It shone smoothly,
and she left a swirling
pattern that I liked, although
I looked and said nothing.
When she stepped down for more
mud she said, "Sometimes

I fix it, sometimes not.
Mostly I fix it—now
in the dry time before rain.
That's good. But sometimes
I say the hell with it,
the rain will only wash it,
the frost crack it, the wind
blow it away. I'm not so
young no more. Well, but mostly
I fix it, I feel better
when I fix it—you know?
I remember my mother."

Celeste Turner Wright:
KINEO MOUNTAIN

Moosehead Lake, Maine

"Pig'back" she brought me where the lake surrounded
That mighty beast, the mountain. I was four,
Delighted to go wading by the shore.
She fed me chicken sandwiches . . . expounded
The mountain's wonders: lead and line had sounded
Vainly the waters near it; furthermore,
Daredevils trained in Switzerland forbore
To try the flint above; they were astounded.

That beach is ugly now with logs—forgotten.
High noon today was not a picnic time:
I shivered, for the wind was full of autumn,
And long ago my mother, past her prime,
Encountered darker lakes that had no bottom,
And other cliffs impossible to climb.

For me a poem begins with my strong emotional response to some person, place, experience, or symbol. "Kineo Mountain" combines all these possibilities. I planned it soon after revisiting a beach on Moosehead Lake, Maine. When I was four years old, my mother carried me "piggyback" through the woods to that beach. After I had gone wading, she told me stories of the mountain and fed me chicken sandwiches. Now, more than half a century later, the resort hotel where my father worked has disappeared; the beach is returning to wilderness; and my mother has died.

The subject of "Kineo Mountain" looked promising. Most people like to watch any mother—a cat, an otter, a bear—feeding her young, playing with them, and teaching them. My mother showed me that our mountain looked like a shaggy beast lying down. She said that its flinty cliffs were too dangerous for even experienced climbers. The lake at its roots was so deep that no plumb line had reached the bottom.

The symbolism for my poem seemed ready-made: wading near the shore might represent childhood; the cliffs were the difficulties of life; the deep, dark water was human sorrow and death. My mother, after a lifetime of service to others, had succumbed to old age and illness.

There was potential appeal to the five senses. For visual images I had the scenery and the two picnickers. For touch or bodily sensation, there were the piggyback ride and the wading. When I read the poem aloud, the four booming rhymewords *surrounded, expounded, astounded,* and *sounded* suggested to me the echoes that came from our mountain when someone shouted or a steamboat whistled.

Though I chose my words primarily for their meaning, I kept on revising the poem until—for some reason—it sounded "right." Upon checking back, I find I unconsciously used many words that alliterate—for example *mighty* and *mountain, lead* and *line, past* and *prime, cliffs* and *climb.* I noticed assonance, the repetition of vowel sounds: *surrounded* and *mountain, vainly* and *trained.* There were rich *r*'s, as in *waters, further-*

more, Switzerland, darker, and *others.* I had not consciously sought these effects; it was like playing the piano by ear.

My material fell naturally into the Italian sonnet form, a favorite of mine: the first eight lines would describe the picnic in midsummer; the last six would contrast it with my lonely return on a chilly October day. Even to the writer who prefers to compose free verse, I recommend practicing the sonnet: its definite structure improves one's skill; the rhymes make the poem easier to remember and quote; and the writer must be concise. With a limit of fourteen lines, you know when you're through!   —C.T.W.

Judith Hemschemeyer:
FIRST LOVE

We fell in love at "Journey for Margaret,"
my mother and I. I was the same age
as Margaret O'Brien, braids and all

and she put her arm on the back of my chair
and touched my head and found the lump
I'd got that morning and forgot I had.

"What's this?" she whispered and I whispered back
I'd cracked my head against the brick wall
of the Savings and Loan walking backwards to school.

And the waves of her giggles washed over me
there in the dark. I had astonished her!
No telling what I'd do next!

But whatever it was, I knew that from then on
what happened between us was just as important
as Margaret O'Brien getting adopted up there on the screen.

79

Cynthia Macdonald:
THE LATE MOTHER

One, two, Buckle my shoe
    To go to Boston.
    The phone call said she was going:
    "She can't last long," but
    The buckle has come off my shoe.
Three, four, Close the door.
    Thread the needle.
    There are tears and I am getting
    Far-sighted.
    Try again.
    Knot the thread and sew the buckle on.
Five, six, Pick up sticks.
    Five years ago she almost set the bed on fire,
    Hiding her cigarette under the blanket
    When the surgeon came.
    He took out her lung.
    I have sewn the buckle on backwards.
    Is she puffing away now, blowing
    Smoke out of her tracheotomy tube
    Like the billboard man
    Who steamed rings over Times Square?
Seven, eight, Don't be late.
    I am ripping off the buckle.
    As soon as I finish I will go.
    I will not be late for the dying. Probably.
    The thread knots binding me to my place.
    My father said to her, "We are going to be late
    For the dinner party." Then she said it
    To her next husband, as if
    The going out must be a struggle.
Nine, ten, Big, fat hen,
    Warm and feathery,
    A nest of softness.

Never was, could not be,
"Teach her to tie her shoes, Mademoiselle.
She can't seem to learn and I must
Dress for the dinner party."
The buckle is on.
I keep the needle threaded in case.

The rhyme is over.
We must leave the nursery
But we are afraid.
I hold her, eighty pounds, in my arms,
Becoming her mother and my own.

Marge Piercy:
RAPE POEM

There is no difference between being raped
and being pushed down a flight of cement steps
except that the wounds also bleed inside.

There is no difference between being raped
and being run over by a truck
except that afterward men ask if you enjoyed it.

There is no difference between being raped
and being bit on the ankle by a rattlesnake
except that people ask if your skirt was short
and why you were out alone anyhow.

There is no difference between being raped
and going head first through a windshield
except that afterward you are afraid
not of cars
but half the human race.

The rapist is your boyfriend's brother.
He sits beside you in the movies eating popcorn.
Rape fattens on the fantasies of the normal male
like a maggot in garbage.

Fear of rape is a cold wind blowing
all of the time on a woman's hunched back.
Never to stroll alone on a sand road through pine woods,
never to climb a trail across a bald
without that aluminum in the mouth
when I see a man climbing toward me.

Never to open the door to a knock
without that razor just grazing the throat.
The fear of the dark side of hedges,
the back seat of the car, the empty house
rattling keys like a snake's warning.
The fear of the smiling man
in whose pocket is a knife.
The fear of the serious man
in whose fist is locked hatred.

All it takes to cast a rapist is seeing your body
as jackhammer, as blowtorch, as adding-machine-gun.
All it takes is hating that body
your own, your self, your muscle that softens to flab.

All it takes is to push what you hate,
what you fear onto the soft alien flesh.
To bucket out invincible as a tank
armored with treads without senses
to possess and punish in one act,
to rip up pleasure, to murder those who dare
live in the leafy flesh open to love.

⤜⤝ The "Rape poem" was written when I was staying in
Missoula, Montana for a week as part of what I think was one
of those academic events entitled something like Ecology and
Literature, or whatever was the fashionable title that year. The
first evening I had suggested that a women's supper be organized. Since I was going to spend a week in that town, I thought
I'd like to find out what life was like for the women living
there. What I heard about was a series of rapes and rape murders that were terrorizing local women and girls.

One woman after another spoke to me about particular
rapes, beatings and murders and how alone each woman

seemed to feel. There was little organized women's movement in Missoula at that time; no rape hot line or crisis center; no one to turn to if you had been raped and survived; no safe houses to run to if you felt threatened on the street. When individual women or delegations of women had gone to talk to the local and state police, they had been treated to jokes and callous dismissal.

That night, feeling exposed and vulnerable in a motel room in this strange town, I could not sleep. I kept thinking about the women's individual fear and how each one seemed to think she alone was frightened and was thus irrational, almost infantile, speaking with shame about her fear as if it were somehow her fault. About four in the morning I began work on the "Rape poem." When I gave my public reading a couple of days later, I had written through several drafts. Afterwards a woman came up to beg for a copy of the poem. I explained it was new and I had no copies. She said that because her twelve-year-old daughter was one of the cases, she wanted to show her the poem; she thought the poem might help. So we sat down at a table and she copied the poem by hand.

Afterwards, before the poem ever made it into book form in *Living in the Open,* it was printed and reprinted about forty times. It just walked off on its own. It seemed to meet a real need. I think it's one of those poems where I have worked to articulate many women's experiences as they have given them to me to make clear back to them.

The poem is addressed mostly, however, to men. In it I want to make a man feel how it is to be a woman in a dangerous society in which the violent abuse of a woman's body against her will is encouraged by the media—films, books, men's magazines—as if it were something to celebrate, in which men are encouraged to fantasize about rape as something every woman really wants, as opposed to an experience that always maims and can kill, body and soul. That is why I wrote this poem.

The poem falls in three sections. The first is a litany of the ways in which rape, stripped of myths, resembles other physical accidents and brutalities. The second concerns the fears, the sharp sense of limits women experience which proceed solely from fear of rape. The third section embodies a brief analysis of how males are taught to think of their bodies and themselves in this society, which encourages attacks on women.

—M.P.

Nikki Giovanni:
EGO TRIPPING

(there may be a reason why)

I was born in the congo
I walked to the fertile crescent and built
  the sphinx
I designed a pryamid so tough that a star
  that only glows every one hundred years falls
  into the center giving divine perfect light
I am bad

I sat on the throne
  drinking nectar with allah
I got hot and sent an ice age to europe
  to cool my thirst
My oldest daughter is nefertiti
  the tears from my birth pains
  created the nile
I am a beautiful woman

I gazed on the forest and burned
  out the sahara desert
  with a packet of goat's meat
  and a change of clothes
I crossed it in two hours

I am a gazelle so swift
  so swift you can't catch me

  For a birthday present when he was three
I gave my son hannibal an elephant
  He gave me rome for mother's day
My strength flows ever on

My son noah built new/ark and
I stood proudly at the helm
  as we sailed on a soft summer day
I turned myself into myself and was
  jesus
  men intone my loving name

  All praises All praises
I am the one who would save

I sowed diamonds in my back yard
My bowels deliver uranium
  the filings from my fingernails are
  semi-precious jewels
  On a trip north
I caught a cold and blew
My nose giving oil to the arab world
I am so hip even my errors are correct
I sailed west to reach east and had to round off
  the earth as I went
  The hair from my head thinned and gold was laid
  across three continents

I am so perfect so divine so ethereal so surreal
I cannot be comprehended
  except by my permission

I mean . . . I . . . can fly
like a bird in the sky . . .

୬ i think any poem worth its salt, if poems can indeed be
salty, should allow the reader to think. this poem is of course
a chronological poem tracing the development of humans
through the movement of black women. i have no feelings that
the poem is exclusive of any one but i wanted to write a sassy
hands-on-the-hips poem from the understanding that i am a
woman and indeed was once a girl. i think it works because
the more you know about anthropology and history the more
you can follow what i am saying; on the other hand you can
be a little child with no previous experiences and catch the joy
of the poem. it goes from the first human bones discovered all
the way to the space age. what has been included is as important to me as what has been excluded. what i strove to do was
show progress, movement, humor and a bit of pride.

this is the most i've ever commented on any poem of mine
since i tend to agree with t.s. eliot when he said a poet was the
last person to know what the poem was/is about.   —N.G.

Marge Piercy:
A WORK OF ARTIFACE

The bonsai tree
in the attractive pot
could have grown eighty feet tall
on the side of a mountain
till split by lightning.
But a gardener
carefully pruned it.
It is nine inches high.

Every day as he
whittles back the branches
the gardener croons,
It is your nature
to be small and cozy,
domestic and weak;
how lucky, little tree,
to have a pot to grow in.
With living creatures
one must begin very early
to dwarf their growth:
the bound feet,
the crippled brain,
the hair in curlers,
the hands you
love to touch.

Sam Cornish:
MONTGOMERY
—for Rosa Parks

white woman have you heard
she is too tired to sit in the back
her feet are two hundred years old

move to the back or walk
around to the side door how
long can a woman be a cow

your feet will not move
and you never listen
but even if it rains empty

seats will ride through town
i walk for my children
my feet two hundred years old

ᑇ My most effective poems bring to personal and autobiographical experience a concrete and specific image, combined
with poetic techniques, and create a logical sequence reflect-
ing the known, universal and historical memory of the reader.

In the poem "Montgomery," my focus is not on the historical or actual person of Rosa Parks. Although the tone is autobiographical, the person is a fictional fragment affirming the
consequences of Parks' action as a literal step toward a reso-
lution in black America:

she is too tired to sit in the back

refers to both a common experience and an oppressive one for
black citizens of Montgomery.

white woman have you heard

makes this a racial incident exposing the inner world of Rosa
Parks as she confronts this without bitterness but with anger.

her feet are two hundred years old

epitomizes the duration of black oppression in history and specifically, Parks' plight as a domestic.

move to the back or walk
around to the side door how
long can a woman be a cow

The implication of the question now directs itself to the white
woman, reaching beyond civil rights into the women's movement of the past and present. The imagery is both personal
(racial) and concrete: side door—concrete; cow—concrete;
empty seats—concrete; children—personal; my feet—personal.

The poem then designates racism as a doctrine which does not recognize gender but permeates the life of the black person beyond the boycott, challenging values which this political but personal act has yet to deal with.

your feet will not move
and you never listen

accuses the white woman who, in spite of their common gender, neither takes action nor listens to Parks as a symbol of the boycott.

but even if it rains empty
seats will ride through town

The image of empty seats and the solitary bus driven through the dark streets of Montgomery on schedule reaffirms Parks' commitment and that of the black people of Montgomery to be heard and to make "you," the white people, listen and concludes:

i walk for my children
my feet two hundred years old

signifying that the boycott is beyond the immediate self interest of the participant: a seat on the bus, front or back, is but a step toward altering the future with a reference to the past ("my feet two hundred years old"). With the affirmative "i walk for my children," Parks vows she will not complain or simply talk: she will take action. The commonplace has now become meaningful and, in retrospect, the reader has experienced the impact of racism and history on Rosa Parks and has learned how Parks has influenced our lives. In December, 1955, Rosa Parks set in motion the Montgomery bus boycott which brought Martin Luther King, Jr. into prominence, officially beginning the Civil Rights Act.   —S.C.

Cynthia Macdonald:
THE LADY PITCHER

It is the last of the ninth, two down, bases loaded, seventh
Game of the Series and here she comes, walking
On water,
Promising miracles. What a relief
Pitcher she has been all year.
Will she win it all now or will this be the big bust which
She secures in wire and net beneath her uniform,
Wire and net like a double
Vision version
Of the sandlot homeplate backstop in Indiana where
She became known as Flameball Millie.

She rears back and fires from that cocked pistol, her arm.
Strike one.
Dom, the catcher, gives her the crossed fingers sign,
Air, but she shakes it off and waits for fire.
Strike two.
Then the old familiar cry, "Show them you got balls, Millie."
But she knows you should strike while the iron is hot
Even though the manager has fined her
Sixteen times for disobeying
The hard and fast one:
A ball after two strikes.
She shoots it out so fast
It draws
An orange stripe on that greensward.
Strike three.

In the locker room they hoist her up and pour champagne
All over her peach satin, lace-frilled robe.
She feels what she has felt before,
The flame of victory and being loved

Moves through her, but this time
It's the Series and the conflagration matches
The occasion.

In the off-season she dreams of victories and marriage,
Knowing she will have them and probably not it.
Men whisper, in wet moments of passion,
"My little Lowestoft," or, "My curvy Spode," and
They stroke her handle, but she is afraid that yielding means
Being filled with milk and put on
The shelf;
So she closes herself off,
Wisecracking.
When she is alone again she looks at the china skin
Of her body, the crazing, the cracks she put there
To make sure
She couldn't
Hold anything for long.

◌ I've been a sports fan since I was a teenager; for two summers I didn't miss a NY Giants (baseball) home game, went to several cities to watch them play, even bribed a dining car waiter to give me Mel Ott's soup bowl. Looking back, I guess I was what would now be called a baseball groupie. In the off-season, I followed pro football and hockey though with less intensity. But this love of spectator sports—which has continued waxing and waning as teams abandoned old home towns and certain sports moved in and out of favor (baseball, out, tennis, football and skating, in)—never surfaced in my poems until "The Lady Pitcher" which really returns to that old beloved turf. A poet friend, Stephen Dunn, told me he was putting together an anthology of sports poems and asked me to contribute something, saying he needed some poems by women. I carried his request around for over a year in that place in my brain where poem ideas lie fallow, then for unknown reasons—such reasons are usually unknown—the idea germinated and out came Flameball Millie. The part of the poem about the Series game and the celebration appeared fairly easily, but what could I follow that with? It took me quite a while longer to find an ending stanza.

One of the tools a poet uses to build a poem is an awareness of all the possible meanings of each word. The context of the word gives us the major meaning, but all the other meanings are there, too, asserting themselves to varying degrees.

For example, the phrase "What a relief pitcher . . ." has as its primary meaning the statement that Millie has been a very good relief pitcher all year, but it also has, emphasized by the line break (another tool poets use), the meaning what a relief it is to have such a pitcher available.

This awareness of the many meanings of words—including puns which I believe are part of the array of meanings, particularly when one *listens* to the poem—gave me the ending I needed. I would use the double-meaning of *pitcher*. I think a star lady pitcher would have a difficult time with her social life, as men would feel threatened by her intrusion into the competitive male world and would either run from her or try to get her to leave baseball to become a housewife and mother. So I suddenly saw her as a china pitcher left on the shelf. But she has worked too hard to get where she is and has made cracks in her skin to make sure she won't give in and accept that fate. She'll hold neither men nor milk for long.

Another probable reason I wrote this poem is that it is one of a long series (not baseball) dealing with performance. I used to be an opera singer and have, therefore, experienced what it means to have to do your very best at one specific moment. That's what performers have to do; one of the pleasures of being a poet is that poets don't. A couple of my poems about performance are included in this book ("The Late Mother," about a daughter and her dying mother, is the other and might be labelled with the phrase, "in the performance of her duties), but I have many more—about tightrope walkers, a man who walks through fire, an orchestra conductor, etc. Performance, I believe, is a metaphor for those moments we all face when we must make crucial decisions quickly, using all the abilities we possess, perhaps even summoning some we didn't know, until that moment of necessity, we had. In that moment our capacities are heightened, as in each successful poem our perceptions are heightened so that we can recognize and delight in something which previously had been just beyond our grasp.

—C.M.

Linda Pastan:
SEPTEMBER

it rained in my sleep
and in the morning the fields were wet

I dreamed of artillery
of the thunder of horses

in the morning the fields were strewn
with twigs and leaves

as if after a battle
or a sudden journey

I went to sleep in summer
I dreamed of rain

in the morning the fields were wet
and it was autumn

⚬ What are dreams anyway? Do we invent them or do they invent us? I carry my dreams around with me all day, as haunted by them as if they had been real events in my life, and maybe they were. In that sense, I suppose, dreams *can* make things happen. In this poem I tried to deal with these random and not altogether logical matters. I suppose on one level you might say that I dreamed of rain because I heard the sound of it even through my sleep and that sometimes it seems as if summer and autumn are only separated by one night. But I hope my small poem also implies something a bit more mysterious, even a bit dangerous. I wrote it all in one day, between waking up and going back to sleep to dream some more. I came to write it because it asked to be written.   —L.P.

Vern Rutsala:
THE WORLD

I move back by shortcut
and dream. I fly above
it all, the dark stain
where swamps soak up
the lake's extravagance,
stubble hills, the valley's
green finger. This is the place
of pure invention, secret
as old wood
under a hundred coats
of paint. I invent
my own way back, invent
these wings, this
Piper Cub of tissue paper
I glide in, circling the valley
chasing my shadow across
the lake, twisting each layer
back through air.
The town scatters out
along the highway and I cut low
buzzing the school, signaling
my old teachers' chalky bones.
I bank away approaching town
along the old road
that rises from a low plain
where the land tastes bad,
where dust even slips
under rich men's doors.
I trace it like a route
on a map and it climbs
kept company by a creek
with a mouth full of boulders.

I finger wind for updrafts
slowing above the dump,
then sweep around the lake,
past Indian Village
and summer homes,
steering hard I top
the mill, my steering wheel
an old lard can lid
on the end of a stick,
my seat a log set back
in the woods, the shade cool
and safe in the arc cut
by the rope swing
thirty years ago.

William Carpenter:
THE KEEPER

I forget everything. I forget faces,
I forget the plots of movies, how
anything turned out, who is divorced
what couples are having an affair.
I am not fit to be alone.
You say I am like the Baron de Charlus
who could never be outside without
his keeper. I should have a keeper,
one of those unsmiling plainclothed men
that forms circles around the President.
He would be physically large, he would
be trained in Chinese methods of restraint
for times when I forgot myself at parties
or began speaking aloud in the public street.
He would have reproducible features; he could

stand in at the annual family picture.
He would remind me of my lectures. In time
he would begin giving the lectures himself
while I sat attentively in the first row.
He would grow rabbinical with learning,
the keeper, he would grow old,
bits of food would appear in his thick beard
like insects; there would be insects
in his beard. He would accept all
my insomnia, he would lie there in the night
recalling the details of my life,
baffled with guilt, baffled with failing
to reach out when things went by.
It would be good sleeping while he stared
into the night. It would be good dreaming
of a simple, phenomenal world,
of the great translucent forms of giraffes.
It would be good to rise, like an idiot,
in a morning totally new, it would be the body
of the keeper beside the door, it would be
his death on the last day and not my own.
It would be I who kept on living here
and kept forgetting.

Richard Eberhart:
FLUX

The old Penobscot Indian
Sells me a pair of moccasins
That stain my feet yellow.

The gods of this world
Have taken the daughter of my neighbor,
Who died this day of encephalitis.

The absentee landlord has taken over Tree Island
Where one now hesitates to go for picnics,
Off the wide beach to see Fiddle Head.

The fogs are as unpredictable as the winds.
The next generation comes surely on,
Their nonchalance baffles my intelligence.

Some are gone for folly, some by mischance,
Cruelty broods over the inexpressible,
The inexorable is ever believable.

The boy, in his first hour on his motorbike,
Met death in a head-on collision.
His dog stood silent by the young corpse.

Last week, the sea farmer off Stonington
Was tripped in the wake of a cruiser.
He went down in the cold waters of the summer.

Life is stranger than any of us expected,
There is a somber, imponderable fate.
Enigma rules, and the heart has no certainty.

Greg Kuzma:
SOMETIMES

I am afraid of being crushed in the pincers
of an enormous dog. I am afraid of
breathing into my lungs the gastric juices
of my own stomach. I fear that the semi-trailer truck
will suddenly blow a tire and come swerving into my own
    lane
and turn my car and my body into a horrible pulp.
I am afraid it will not be quick enough when it happens.
I am afraid as well of lingering dying, living at the
edge of a cliff and the long hurt ache up the arms,
the bowels distended out through the anus, or the
lungs growing feathery and faint, crinkling up like
wax paper after the sandwich is removed.
I am afraid, at night, sometimes, of arising from bed
and smashing my shin on the weight set bar I have on
the floor by the edge of the bed, of the bone bruising,
and the lump rising up.
I am afraid of the fall down stairs, with the back
bone trying to right itself, the head trying to get
pointed in the right direction, but the body falling
like a child into a pool relaxed on a hot day,
only the arms breaking off in the posts of the railing.
I am afraid of having my skull crushed under the plate
of an enormous press which someone is lowering
a fraction of an inch at a time, of the skull cracking
first like a walnut shell, and the momentary relief,
of the eyes growing milky and then popping out,
staring back up briefly upon the twisted face, the
teeth pinned against each other, then splintering,
the facial bones breaking through the skin like a
wrecked ship coming up from the placid bottom
where all these years its rigging was a place for fish

to swim through, and the blood of course and the
squirting brains. I am afraid as well even to
look upon such things happening to others, afraid
to get out of the car at the roadside last week
when the big green pickup truck went over on its side,
and there was inside the cab the person jumping up and
    down
trying to get out, like a frog in a jar. I am afraid
of the fingers of cancer touching touching, or
pneumonia which floods the lungs with phlegm, or
the coughing fit which brings the stomach up, the tubes
to the back of the throat. I am afraid of the stench
of the body, the little whisps from the anus, the
gagging gargle breath of the old. I am afraid
that someday in front of a building someone will jump
upon me and snap my back like a twig and I go jostling
to the ground, dancing, jerking in a kind of sexual spasm.
Or that a knife will be inserted under my left breast
and like a zipper drawn across my chest while someone
says, as in the film THE GODFATHER, this is for you my
    friend.
I am afraid for the big soft belly I hide under shirts,
that it will be ripped open and the insides yanked out
and burned in front of me, as used to be done nearly every
    week
or so in other civilized cultures. I am afraid for the ribs
that they will not be strong against the huge priers,
and that the heart will shrivel like a prune at a single touch.
I think of myself often on line with the beeves
waiting to be stuck or jabbed with the current,
the brain to sizzle up suddenly like a toaster short circuit,
and the whole body, once so quick and light, to fall like a
bag of mud onto the slimed floor. Or to do that
to other living things, to hook them and lift them
dazed onto a belt of bodies, to slice them open like butter

with hot knives, to peel them like bananas. I am
afraid that a bullet will come like a jet plane
right up the front of my face, right up a nostril
and take out the whole back of my skull and its contents,
and that it not be quick enough. Or that I might be
even in some dream impaled on a stake, feeling it rise
up through my rectum, up beside the lungs and out around
the left shoulder, and my hands bound and numb.
Or of having my throat ripped out by some vicious dog.
I am afraid that my hands will be hacked off by a big man
wearing a lumberjack shirt, first the left hand
and then the right, and that I will be then asked
to walk all the way home, looking down at my arms
and out again at the world, the butterflies, the lawn
    sprinklers
spinning their little silver cornets.

∞ In many of my poems I am caught up in sounds and
rhythms. Generally, in fact, rhythm is what generates my
poems. I hear something which begins to select words, which
then urge upon me the logic or reason with which I begin to
understand how the poem has to go, how it must develop.
Often I have tried to characterize my procedure as being essen-
tially musical and imitative. A person has a guitar which he
carries about. Street sounds and bird song and very much also
the sounds of other guitars and other musics stir him to re-
spond, or make him want to initiate his own melodies. Sometimes it is copying, or answering, or starting where something
has left off prematurely.

In the poem "Sometimes," however, I am trying to write
more or less directly out of images of pain and damage which
are everywhere around me and which intercept me often.
Rather than let a rhythm take over and shape my words I tried
to write a plain and matter of fact prose which might deliver,

without indirection or distraction, some of these nightmarish images. Admittedly within the lines I myself become distracted by both the possibility of sounds and rhythms, and this is as it should be if one is going to get any help with his writing.

Part of the impulse to write a poem like "Sometimes" must rest with the notion of preventing such things from occurring through imagining them in advance. It is a desire to bring what is mostly subconcious into some kind of open area where these things may even be seen to be less terrible than they at first seem. Also a poem like "Sometimes" acts as a kind of release, a kind of confession, the burden of these fears having been lifted off into the words.   —G.K.

Celeste Turner Wright:
NOBLESSE OBLIGE

("high-born persons have obligations")

Why is the princess so depressed
Since Frog retrieved her ball
And hopped as a triumphant guest
Into her father's hall:

Like darkened lenses gleamed the well;
But when the royal maid
Gazed where the golden bauble fell,
He goggled upward from his cell
And bartered her his aid.

Now throat abubble near her plate
And green legs folded by her chair,
Beside her tapestry or lute,
The visitor is there;

Patient on bedroom rug will wait
In fringe of counterpane
Where little shoes are toeing out
Ready to walk again.

Plague on the promise lightly got
That binds her though she wince!
Banish the tantalizing thought
That miracles could change her lot:
Sometimes a frog becomes a prince . . .
But often he does not.

William Carpenter:
FIRE

This morning, on the opposite shore of the river,
I watch a man burning his own house.
It is a cold day, and the man wears thick gloves
and a fur hat that gives him a Russian look.
I envy his energy, since I am still on the veranda
in my robe, with morning coffee, my day not
even begun, while my neighbor has already piled
spruce boughs against his house and poured
flammable liquids over them to send a finger
of black smoke into the air, a column surrounded
by herring gulls, who think he's having a barbecue
or has founded a new dump. I hadn't known what labor
it took to burn something. Now the man is working
at such speed, he's like the criminal in a silent
movie, as if he had a deadline, as if he had
to get his house burned by a certain time, or it
would be all over. I see his kids helping, bringing
him matches and kindling, and I'd like to help out

myself, I'd like to bring him coffee and a bagel,
but the Penobscot river separates us, icebergs
the size of small ships drifting down the tide.
Moreover, why should I help him when I have a house
myself, which needs burning as much as anyone's?
It has begun to leak. I think it has carpenter ants.
I hear them making sounds at night like writing, only
they aren't writing, they are building small tubular
cities inside the walls. I start burning in the study,
working from within so it will go faster, so I can
catch up, and soon there's a smoke column on either
shore, like a couple of Algonquins having a dialogue
on how much harder it is to destroy than to create.
I shovel books and poems into the growing fire. If
I burn everything, I can start over, with a future
like a white rectangle of paper. Then I notice
my neighbor has a hose, that he's spraying his house
with water, the coward, he has bailed out, but I
keep throwing things into the fire: my stamps,
my Berlioz collection, my photos of nude people,
my correspondence dating back to grade school.
Over there, the fire engines are reaching his home.
His wife is crying with relief, his fire's extinguished.
He has walked down to the shore to see the ruins
of the house across the river, the open cellar,
the charred timbers, the man laughing and dancing
in the snow, who has been finally freed from his
possessions, who has no clothes, no library, who has
gone back to the beginning, when we lived in nature:
no refuge from the elements, no fixed address.

෴ I wrote the poem "Fire" just after hearing that a friend
of mine watched his house burn down on New Year's Day,
1982. I had heard that some aboriginal tribe made a ceremony

of burning all their possessions, houses, furniture, every year getting rid of the old to make room for the new. I thought it was horrible that my friend's house burned, but also that it was a new beginning. He could start his life over. I was of two minds about it, and that led to the two men in the poem, one who is timid and fails to go through with it, calls the fire department; the other who goes all the way and burns it down. I'm sure I was both of those people, the radical and the conservative.

Many of my poems are about two people who are really one, like all the "doubles" in literature, Dr. Jekyll and Mr. Hyde. Yeats said that all good poetry is about the "quarrel with the self," and the reader looks in on that argument through the window of the poem. "The Keeper" is on the same theme, a man who invents a double for himself, an alter ego, like a stunt man who would stand in for him in social situations, and in the end stand in when it's time to die.

After I wrote "Fire" and read it over, I saw other things, not "intended" while writing the poem, but which got into it subliminally, a kind of political meaning. These could be two countries facing each other. I guess I suggest this by "the hat which gives him a Russian look" though at the time I was just thinking of a Russian-style fur hat. Maybe this is the foolishness of the superpowers, also, trapped in a competition to see which nation can destroy itself first. I know I was thinking about the arms race the winter I wrote this poem. The futility of all envy and competition comes through in the poem, but there's also some glory in it. It scares me to think how much this man *gets into* self-destruction, throwing his things into the fire. He's a fanatic; the man across the river is saner, more temperate, maybe more boring in the long run. They are certainly two of the ways you can approach an experience.

People ask, "Does a poet really intend all this meaning in a poem?" During the act of writing some things creep in subconsciously, which the poet sees later and emphasizes during the stages of revision. "Fire" was probably rewritten twenty or thirty times, till it seemed right. By the time the revisions are done, the poet has considered almost every conceivable meaning in the poem, though he is still often surprised and delighted by what other people see in the poem—sometimes things he never even dreamed of until they are pointed out. In this way, the act of reading a poem becomes just about as creative as the act of writing it.   —W.C.

Joyce Carol Oates:
THE SUICIDE

didn't acknowledge receipt
didn't wave goodbye
didn't flutter the air with kisses
a mound of tinsel gifts unwrapped
air mail letters unopened
bedclothes rumpled
No thank you

always elsewhere

though it was raining elsewhere
though strange-speaking persons peopled the streets
the minarets might have been dangerous
the drinking water suspect
though we at home slaved and baked
and wept and dialed the phone
and hung tinsel ornaments
did he marvel
did he thank

was he grateful   did he know
was he considerate
was he human
was he there

Always elsewhere!
didn't thank
didn't kiss
toothbrush stiffened
cat scratching at the screen
car battery dead

was that human?

Went where?

∽ This poem, a favorite of my own among my poetry, addressed itself to the mingled hurt, anger, shock, and incalculable grief survivors feel when someone close to them has committed suicide. The language reflects this stupefication—it's dazed, spare, repetitive, atonic. Like all survivors in this context, the speaker has only questions—questions without answers. (I wrote the poem for obvious reasons . . . and my questions remain unanswered.)   —J.C.O.

Mark Vinz:
VARIATIONS ON A THEME

1
This morning
my child dances naked
in front of the mirror,
unashamed,

unafraid of growing old.
Her face is as thin
as her breakfast egg shell,
looking toward me
huddled between bed sheets.
When she leaves the room
the image keeps dancing
in the mirror.

2
Important decisions today:
clean sheets, the price
of hamburger, where the line
is to be broken,
how to continue.
At the supermarket
I watch a woman beat her child
with a package of celery.
He has broken a jar of applesauce,
while dancing in the aisles.

3
This evening there are fireworks
and dancers in the park.
Behind the crowd,
the old ones
who will not leave their benches
clap their hands together,
even though they cannot see,
even though they cannot be heard.

∾ A few years ago I found myself writing a poem about dancing, probably because one of my closest friends was a dancer. But the poem failed—I really didn't know anything about dancing! But somehow I couldn't let the poem go (or it wouldn't let me go), and when I started work on it again the images came from my own life, my own experiences. It was a long poem, filled with connections and explanations—which ultimately had to be cut away. I was left with three images centering on dancing, and I finally decided to let the reader make his or her own connections between the images. It seems to me that this is the process of most poetry. The writer has to learn to say less and less, to let the imagination make the important discoveries—even if it means writing a poem in sections and giving up on finding a very exciting title.   —M.V.

Richard Shelton:
CERTAIN CHOICES

My friend, who was a heroin addict,
is dead and buried beneath trash
and broken bottles in a prison field.

He died, of course, because of the way
he lived. It wasn't a very good way,
but it kept him alive. When it couldn't
keep him alive any longer, it killed him.
Thoroughly and with great suffering.

After he had made certain choices,
there were no others available. That's
the way it is with certain choices,
and we are faced with them so young.

I have few friends, and none of them
are replaceable. That's the way it is
with friends. We make certain choices.

William Stafford:
PEACE WALK

We wondered what our walk should mean,
taking that un-march quietly;
the sun stared at our signs—"Thou shalt not kill."

Men by a tavern said, "Those foreigners . . ."
to a woman with a fur, who turned away—
like an elevator going down, their look at us.

111

Along a curb, their signs lined across,
a picket line stopped and stared
the whole width of the street at ours: "Unfair."

Above our heads the sound truck blared—
by the park, under the autumn trees—
it said that love could fill the atmosphere:

Occur, slow the other fallout, unseen,
on islands everywhere—fallout, falling
unheard. We held our poster up to shade our eyes.

At the end we just walked away;
no one was there to tell us where to leave the signs.

You could tell about something that actually happens. Don't make up anything, at first. Just tell it. You will not tell *everything*. That is impossible. But you tell what seems most helpful to tell, what you think about when you remember.

Then you could go back and take out the things that do not help on the main track of the events. Don't try ahead of time to decide what will be important: trust your feelings, let them guide you.

Surprise! Actuality has many riches in it. What happens to happen has stray elements, but it also has cohesive bits—and the cohesiveness is why you remember certain parts and slight other parts.

I went on a peace march. Then I told about it. I couldn't put in some of the things—they would distract, or sound artificial (one student was carrying a paperback "Works of Aristotle"—I liked that, but I didn't think readers would believe me). And I wanted them to believe, and to see how important our march was, and is. And how there are some burdens you always carry, and there isn't anyone who can tell you to put them down.   —W.S.

Thom Gunn:
THE IDEA OF TRUST

The idea of trust, or,
the thief. He
was always around,
'pretty' Jim.
Like a lilac bush or
a nice picture on the wall.
Blue eyes of an
intense vagueness
and the well-arranged
bearing of an animal.
Then one day he
said something!
                he said
that trust is
an intimate conspiracy.

What did that
mean? Anyway next day
he was gone, with
all the money and dope
of the people he'd lived with.

I begin
to understand. I see him
picking through their things
at his leisure, with
a quiet secret smile
choosing and taking,
having first discovered
and set up his phrase to
scramble
that message of
enveloping trust.

He's getting
free. His eyes
are almost transparent.
He has put on
gloves. He fingers
the little privacies of those
who acted as if there
should be no privacy.

They took that
risk.
    Wild lilac
chokes the garden.

∞ This poem was based on an incident of a few years ago,
in the early seventies. I lived in the lower half of a two-story
house. Upstairs was the other apartment, and at that time it
was like a permanent party. Not so inconvenient as it might
sound: you could dip in and out whenever you wanted, as it
seemed I was welcome. People stayed up there from periods
varying between a night and a month. One day one of the
permanent residents came down and told me that money had
been stolen. "Do you know who did it?" I asked. "Yes," she
said, "Jim."—"*Which* Jim?" I said. "Oh you know," she said,
"*pretty* Jim."

Yes, I knew Pretty Jim. He just sat around, never saying
much, though whether because he was shy or dumb or just
plain burned out I didn't know. But then after all this I heard
from another person about a conversation Jim had had up
there, before he took the money, in which he had been most
articulate. It was in this conversation that he had made his
definition of trust, which I came to realize said more about his
state of mind than about trust itself. He felt conspired against;
and stealing was his way of getting free, of establishing his
separateness.

But I didn't get that at once. There are many possible things that start the itch in my mind that can finally only be made to go away by writing. The itch in this case was one of puzzlement. I puzzled and puzzled about his reported definition of trust, and the poem was perhaps an attempt to understand. What surprised me when I read the poem through (and it wasn't written quickly, but over a period of weeks), was that through that attempt of the imagination I had ended up being a little sympathetic to the thief, which I certainly hadn't been before. So maybe writing poetry *is* good for the soul.

The poem begins like the title of a moralistic Victorian children's book, e.g. *Eric, or, Little by Little.*   —T.G.

David McElroy:
NOCTURN AT THE INSTITUTE

This black scrap from Viet Nam,
deaf paraplegic, wheels off
the basketball court with nine equal
friends. They drive their own electric
chairs.

He knows that we think the sad should not
be cruel. In the room reserved for helping them,
he writes on paper, Tell me
just what dying is, you faggot,
ok, buddy?

Well, I guess
it is sitting a lot, for the man who can't walk.
It is world news, for the Soldiers' Home.
My liberal views on women, for women.
It is silence, for the blind.
For example, a handful of wool
landing in a pan filled with snow.
It is nothing, nothing at all,
for the cabbage down the hall.

Mike Lowery:
NAM

no one wants to hear about the war
—not the true stories anyway

it's all cowboy's newsreels and
Audie Murphy heroes

never the chain saw bite of AK-47's
under the blinding Chu Lai sun
or chopper rides over tin roofed towns
to blood-red landing pads

where medics save me from
the cutting room floor
and make me into a memento
to remind me that
arms and legs can't be
spliced from old MGM movies

Hayden Carruth:
WHEN HOWITZERS BEGAN

When howitzers began
    the fish darted downward
to weeds and rocks,
    dark forms motionless
in darkness, yet they were
    stunned and again
stunned
    and again and
again stunned, until their
    lives loosened, spreading
a darker darkness
    over the river.

❧ "When Howitzers Began" was one of a number of poems
I wrote during the war in Vietnam. Like so many other mil-
lions of people, I was dismayed and outraged by the suffering
inflicted on that little nation, and for me the suffering included

what was felt by the animals and trees and rice paddies as much as the pain of human beings. (One of my poems was called "The Birds of Viet-nam.") I meant nothing more by this than the fact that for me all living things are parts—equal parts—of this earth's population.

I don't remember when the poem was written exactly. I'm not much good at keeping records. But I remember it was at a time when the state department of parks in Vermont destroyed the fish in Lake Elmore by detonating huge explosive charges under the water. I don't know why this was done; presumably the authorities believed that the fish population had become too large or perhaps too polluted. Big fish floated to shore belly up. Bass, sturgeon, lake trout, etc. Because I had Vietnam on my mind continually in those days, I immediately thought of the fish over there, how they too could be stunned to death by the explosions of artillery shells, even by shells that did not land in the rivers. (I believe, though I am not certain, that at some time before I wrote the poem I had read an account of conditions in Vietnam which included this information.)

For me, rivers are always dark. They always suggest the aspects of existence that are mysterious and troubling: the passage of time, inevitability, the remorselessness of history.

I tried to arrange the phrasings and line-endings in my poem so that the reader would be forced to *hear* the irregular but repeated detonations of the artillery shells. And in the visual imagery of the poem I tried to work with the various shades of darkness to suggest, as the river itself becomes darker by the loosening of the dark blood, the dark "souls," of the fishes, not only sorrow, not only evil, but the cruel mindlessness of the whole event. Of course it is not for me to say if the poem succeeds; but when I have included it in my public readings, people have often told me they were much moved by it.

It is a small poem, a slight poem. I think perhaps it does what most small poems are intended to do: it creates a momentary insight and feeling in the reader's mind, which is soon forgotten but which lingers in the reader's subconsciousness long afterward, thus affecting his or her life indefinitely. Perhaps—who knows?—it may even produce a very minor but significant change in some people's personalities. —H.C.

W. D. Snodgrass:
TEN DAYS LEAVE

He steps down from the dark train, blinking; stares
At trees like miracles. He will play games
With boys or sit up all night touching chairs.
Talking with friends, he can recall their names.

Noon burns against his eyelids, but he lies
Hunched in his blankets; he is half awake
But still lacks nerve to open up his eyes;
Supposing it were just his old mistake?

But no; it seems just like it seemed. His folks
Pursue their lives like toy trains on a track.
He can foresee each of his father's jokes.
Like words in some old movie that's come back.

He is like days when you've gone some place new
To deal with certain strangers, though you never
Escape the sense in everything you do,
'We've done this all once. Have I been here, ever?'

But no; he thinks it must recall some old film, lit
By lives you want to touch; as if he'd slept
And must have dreamed this setting, peopled it,
And wakened out of it. But someone's kept

His dream asleep here like a small homestead
Preserved long past its time in memory
Of some great man who lived here and is dead.
They have restored his landscape faithfully:

The hills, the little houses, the costumes:
How real it seems! But he comes, wide awake,
A tourist whispering through the priceless rooms
Who must not touch things or his hand might break

Their sleep and black them out. He wonders when
He'll grow into his sleep so sound again.

Frank Steele:
GREENER GRASS

I was born in the city
and have always been
too easy to reach by phone.
Traffic goes by all the time
bumper to bumper, days
of chrome and nights
full of headlights
inside me. I used to hate it
but there you are.

My father was raised in the country
and lives there still, although
long since moved to the city.
Nothing gets to him behind
masses of reserve, old ways
up from the fields or once a week
down chert roads to the post office
wearing a hat that he still tips
to people in the dust of maybe
one car coming.

He envies me still from a distance
no phone can reach or car
connect. Even at this late date,
learning to live my life in traffic,
I wish I could tell him what it meant
once to see the sun come up
across his fields.

Barbara Howes:
RETURNING TO STORE BAY

Coming back to this generous island—
Shore, harbor, beach—
Is to leave behind images blown
Like cats through a shadow alley,
    And the feel of cement in the teeth . . .

Returning to Store Bay
One comes back to the circular sound
Of wind whacking the scrolled
Water, the vast contest
    Of undertow and surf;

To the savage ironing
Of breezes, rolling on out, stropping,
Whaling, pulling back in, the water
Huge in some artisan hand;
    Surf and wind are round.

—In a ferryslip, wings
Of brown paper from a subway
Kiosk play hopscotch, stretch out
In gutters of that town whose
    Sidewalks abrade the throat.—

Coming back to this bay
Is to meet again the guffawing
Ocean, is to dance, dimensional,
Hewed out by wind, in the round,
    Alive in the muscular sea.

挓 "Returning to Store Bay" makes a rather clear contrast
between the reality of an island bay, and that of the cramped

and cluttered streets of some cities. Store Bay is, indeed, a wonderfully generous beach on the island of Tobago in the Caribbean, and we have had the good fortune to be able to "return" there several times; "Returning" being infinitely more satisfying than "Arriving" would be. I therefore go on to alternate brief views of both worlds as the poem continues.

To read poetry with most benefit and pleasure, one must read with the eye, of course, but also *hear* it. Repeat it aloud to yourself, so as to take in how important *sound* is in language; how wonderfully the music can in some mysterious way add to and deepen the meaning. Some words, too, have much more suggestive power than others; are more complex, more moving. Reading a poem is not like reading a birthday card— not that that is not a pleasure too: it becomes, in the best poetry, truly an experience. Of course it is only fair to say that while we were overcome with delight at being back at Store Bay, there must have been some Tobagans on the beach who were busy thinking how they would really like to ride in a subway! —*B.H.*

Frank Steele:
COUNTRY GREETING

The hand goes up
that cranks the tractor
and stacks bales.

The hand at a glance is full of work.
At noon in the middle of July
callouses hover over something growing
not far from the graves of warriors.
Work is a kind of violence.
Violence is speed and weight, a digging
thought of by the body and spoken with the hands.

The violence of work comes to live
in callouses that are like little graves
on the rich plain of the palm.

Out here anything can happen.
And so the farmer smiles going by
and waggles his graves at me.

⧠ One summer recently I took off and lived in the deep
south for a couple of months, taking the family. We were in a
small house a few miles outside the city. I noticed that when I
drove down a country road, the person I was meeting—often
in a truck carrying vegetables or lumber—would throw up his
hand in greeting. Probably everyone who has lived in relative
isolation but with a car has noticed this phenomenon. It doesn't
happen in cities, where irritable drivers sometimes give other
kinds of hand-gestures. "Country Greeting" began, as most of
my poems do, in an effort to explore and clarify something
that occurred to me that I didn't know the answer to.

I knew that the farmer's throwing up his hand to me in
greeting as we passed on the road had a connection with the
fact that we were both isolated but having a brief, anonymous
encounter. I knew it also had a connection with the countryside that we were both inhabiting, the activities that typically
go on there and the dangers that sometimes accompany them.
Farmers are people, usually, with enormous energy, a sense of
discipline and commitment to a way of life. They deal every
day with the problem of controlling the external world. If successful in their work, they are very good at repairing plumbing
and electricity, landscaping, putting on roofs, painting, and a
thousand other things that happen outside the self. What they
do for an interior life is a more complex question, and I took
the farmer's greeting as the beginning of an affirmative answer
to it—only a signal, and yet a stoic and lonely moment of re-
assurance.

For me, an awareness of landscape is never very far from an awareness of mortality, and some of that feeling came into the poem. I hadn't planned for the poem to make a circle, but I see now that it does, beginning with an upraised hand, going off into a little meditation in the middle, and coming back to the hand at the end—but maybe with a difference.   —F.S.

Mark Vinz:
OLD DOC

His gimpy leg was testimony to
some other surgeon's art—
he was the best, though he'd never
tell you that.

He drove a big green oldsmobile
until his hands started shaking—
there were some folks who could
never forgive him that—
not the car, the hands,
the drinks he'd take each day
down at the Sportsman Bar
just to pass the time between
the mail box and his empty office
over the grocery store.
What these folks forget could fill
an elevator bin—
the horse and buggy days,
the times he sweated through a blizzard
to deliver a baby on a failing farm
somewhere so far out in the sticks
you'd need a compass and a prayer to find it.
With spring thaw those farmers
brought him sacks of potatoes from

their cellar holes, and jars of
pickled beets and corn.
Money? Hell, there wasn't any left,
but he stayed on, and when the
Valley City clinic started up
the town folks left him for it,
just like flies to a new corpse.

Sure, he was the best.
And now there's not a doctor living
within 30 miles of here—
nor was there when *his* stroke came around.

Doug Cockrell:
FIELD WORK

On his last swing around
what I saw was the smoke
stack of his tractor, his head
rising over a sloped field,
the sun around, his body
flexed above the plow, pulling
open the ground for
whatever rain or sun was
coming to him.

He went down that way—
one leg dangling;
tripped up his plow and drove
through the west fence gate standing up

—into the clutter of his farmyard;
shut up the hogs; had a second thought:
dropped a tin can over the smoke stack.

126

Karl Shapiro:
GARAGE SALE

Two ladies sit in the spotless driveway
Casually smoking at the not-for-sale card table,
Over their heads a row of plastic pennants,
Orange, yellow, assorted reds and blues,
Such as flap over used-car lots, a symbol.
Each thing for sale is hand-marked with a label,
And every object shows its homemade bruise.

They sit there all day, sometimes getting up
When a visitor asks a question about a crib
Or a box spring with a broken rib
Or a gas jet to start fireplace fires.

Cars park gently, some with daisy decals,
No Mark IV's, Coupe de Villes or Corvettes;
Mostly wagons with the most copious interiors,
And few if any intellectuals.

All day the shoppers in low-key intensities,
Hoping to find something they are trying to remember
Fits in, or sticks out, approach and mosey,
Buy a coffee mug with a motto, or leave,
And nobody introduces him or herself by name.
That is taboo. And nobody walks fast. That is taboo.
And those who come look more or less the same.

A child buys a baby dress for her Raggedy Anns.
A pair of andirons, a mono hi-fi, a portable
    typewriter, square electric fans,
Things obsolescing but not mature enough to be antiques,
And of course paintings which were once expensive
Go or can go for a song.

127

This situation, this neighborly implosion,
As flat as the wallpaper of Matisse
Strikes one as a cultural masterpiece.
In this scene nothing serious can go wrong.

⤳ Most of my poetry since I began has to do with the pe-
culiarly American. More specifically middleclass American,
which is what I know and appreciate best. Now can one imagine a garage sale in France? A flea-market, yes, but a garage
sale? Or in Germany or England or Italy?

At the end of the poem I advance my personal or you might
say moral comment on my subject, an old-fashioned poetic device which I like and use a lot. In my "moral" I say that this
American invention is peaceful, harmless, quiet and *abstract,*
like the more abstract paintings of Matisse, one of my favorite
painters. His paintings are full of interiors and Outside is usually outside the window. He always painted the wallpaper and
that frequently dominates everything else, including the nude
women. The design of the wallpaper becomes the theme. And
I see the garage sale, which I am watching from across the
street (from inside my house) as an abstraction of middleclass
American life. The garage sale is orderly, rhythmical, with the
etiquette of a new and friendly people. (Americans like to meet
strangers.) If I could paint I would paint the garage sale. Being
a word person I write a poem.

The paintings sold at the garage sale are either reproduc-
tions or junk. But a garage sale is not a junk sale: everything
has a further, perhaps final use.

The sale is conducted by ladies; they probably wear dresses.
The cars are rather anonymous, low-key. The money transac-
tion is practically invisible, inaudible. The garage sale is more
for pleasure than business.

The bulk of the poem is built upon the significant objects. I
would like a non-American to *see* what a garage sale is. (I

often think of my poems as being addressed to alien readers. I am guiding them through my particular America. I want them to understand it and like it. I am a patriot.)

The poem is somewhat heavily rhymed. Most of the rhymes are ironic. The poem is also somewhat heavily metered, but inexactly, using the famous decasyllabic line in a vestigial, even nostalgic sense.   —K.S.

Philip Booth:
HOW TO SEE DEER

Forget roadside crossings.
Go nowhere with guns.
Go elsewhere your own way,

lonely and wanting. Or
stay and be early:
next to deep woods

inhabit old orchards.
All clearings promise.
Sunrise is good,

and fog before sun.
Expect nothing always;
find your luck slowly.

Wait out the windfall.
Take your good time
to learn to read ferns;

make like a turtle:
downhill toward slow water.
Instructed by heron,

drink the pure silence.
Be compassed by wind.
If you quiver like aspen

trust your quick nature:
let your ear teach you
which way to listen.

You've come to assume
protective color; now
colors reform to

new shapes in your eye.
You've learned by now
to wait without waiting;

as if it were dusk
look into light falling:
in deep relief

things even out. Be
careless of nothing. See
what you see.

⌒ Since a poet often finds that the finished poem displaces
the experience which moved him to write, it's often hard for
the poet to say how a poem came into being. But I do, even
with the writing far behind me, still know something about the
way "How To See Deer" began. And about the way that writing it led me to see that the poem was not just about deer.

After a year when I saw fawns all summer, and does and
bucks all through hunting season, I realized sometime the next
September that I hadn't, for months, seen even one deer. As I
started the poem that "How To See Deer" finally became, I
think, looking back, that I was trying to write myself instructions on where and how to look for deer, instructions on how
to recover some of my previous years' experience. I think I
may have envisioned the poem as a kind of ironic Field Guide.
But as I got into writing the poem, I found it wanting to move
(and my wanting to let it move) in another direction. I found
myself revising *as I wrote,* until I saw that my revisions were
not focused on looking for deer, but were looking into what I

might, in the abstract, now call something like "access to vision." But when I was writing the poem I wasn't thinking abstractly at all; I was searching for how specifics interrelated.

When the poem was published in *Available Light*, a reviewer wrote that "How To See Deer" gives "explicit advice on how to come to our senses," that it blends "the cryptic directives of Frost, the waylessness of Zen consciousness, and the protective coloring of Thoreau." That strikes me as being right; in retrospect I can sense that the poem contains some of my literary as well as back-country experience. I'm grateful to the reviewer for reminding me of what I wasn't at all conscious of as I was actually writing. As I've been writing this postscript to the poem, I've just now realized how deeply "How To See Deer" is related to earlier poems of mine like "Heron." But just as I've come to that realization only in writing this, so do I know what I similarly discovered in writing "How To See Deer." I found myself finding, as I wrote, that the poem was looking into what I barely knew I was searching for: not deer but ways of being, ways of learning to see.   —*P.B.*

John Tagliabue:
AN UNSEEN DEER

An unseen deer through seen shadows leaps through my heart
A seen deer through unseen songs leaps through winter
And spring, the shadow on the cold dawn, the green beginning,
Ending, leaping, singing, all are in his luminosity.
The King quietly sees us, his eyes swift stars in the leaves,
Blesses us with his power, and then the forest hides him and sings.

Howard Nemerov:
TREES

To be a giant and keep quiet about it,
To stay in one's own place;
To stand for the constant presence of process
And always to seem the same;
To be steady as a rock and always trembling,
Having the hard appearance of death
With the soft, fluent nature of growth,
One's Being deceptively armored,
One's Becoming deceptively vulnerable;
To be so tough, and take the light so well,
Freely providing forbidden knowledge
Of so many things about heaven and earth
For which we should otherwise have no word—
Poems or people are rarely so lovely,
And even when they have great qualities
They tend to tell you rather than exemplify
What they believe themselves to be about,
While from the moving silence of trees,
Whether in storm or calm, in leaf and naked,
Night or day, we draw conclusions of our own,
Sustaining and unnoticed as our breath,
And perilous also—though there has never been
A critical tree—about the nature of things.

Celeste Turner Wright:
THUMBPRINT

California

Almost reluctant, we approach the block
Cleft from a stout sequoia; calculate
By arches, loops, concentric rings the date
Of Hastings, Plymouth, Gettysburg; the shock
Darkens our eyes. As dying men a clock,
We read the scornful summary of fate—
Elizabeth an inch—and estimate
How it will scant our chronicle and mock.

Redwood has fingerprinted Time, the seams
Of his gigantic thumb: a circle grew
With padres' grapevines; when this curve was new,
The miners waded California streams.
Can all our aspirations and our dreams
Leave but a filamentous line or two?

Thom Gunn:
THE CHERRY TREE

In her gnarled sleep it
begins
        though she seems
as unmoving as the statue
of a running man: her
branches caught in a
writhing, her trunk
leaning as if in mid-fall.
When the wind moves

134

against her grave body
only the youngest twigs
scutter amongst themselves.

But there's something going on
in those twisted brown limbs,
it starts as a need
and it takes over, a need
to push
            push outward
from the center, to
bring what is not
from what is, pushing
till at the tips of the push
something comes about
                        and then
pulling it from outside
until yes she has them started
tiny bumps
appear at the ends of twigs.

Then at once they're all here,
she wears them like a coat
a coat of babies,
I almost think that she
preens herself, jubilant at
the thick dazzle of bloom,
that the caught writhing has become
a sinuous wriggle of joy
beneath her fleece.
But she is working still
to feed her children,
there's a lot more yet,
bringing up all she can
a lot of goodness from roots

while the petals drop.
The fleece is gone
as suddenly as it came
and hundreds of babies are left
almost too small to be seen
but they fatten, fatten, get pink
and shine among her leaves.

Now she can repose a bit
they are so fat.
                    She cares less
birds get them, men
pick them, human children wear them
in pairs over their ears
she loses them all.
That's why she made them,
to lose them into the world, she
returns to herself,
she rests, she doesn't care.

She leans into the wind
her trunk shines black
with rain, she sleeps
as black and hard as lava.
She knows nothing about babies.

John Tagliabue:
THE BARE ARMS OF TREES

Sometimes when I see the bare arms of trees in the evening
I think of men who have died without love,
Of desolation and space between branch and branch,
I think of immovable whiteness and lean coldness and fear

And the terrible longing between people stretched apart as
    these branches
And the cold space between.
I think of the vastness and courage between this step and that
    step
Of the yearning and fear of the meeting, of the terrible desire
    held apart.
I think of the ocean of longing that moves between land and
    land
And between people, the space and ocean.
The bare arms of the trees are immovable, without the play of
    leaves, without the sound of wind;
I think of the unseen love and the unknown thoughts that
    exist between tree and tree
As I pass these things in the evening, as I walk.

On being asked to select a few of my thousand poems
for a new Anthology and being asked to say something about
writing them . . .

How shall I say, how shall I choose? I have to write poems,
I'm doing that often. It's my freedom. It's my song coming to
terms with the moment—a picture I'm seeing, a bird I am
hearing, the death of my father, the snow falling. My song,
part of the Complete Music, has to make sense, make sentences (or ritual or play) of it, the other soul. Poetry: soul coming to terms via words, that's what's meant by the sacredness
of communication; I find it most practical and necessary. It
alerts me. Writing it down, the song's apprehension of the
event. Even if it is about pain this activity constitutes some sort
of freedom. Freedom in really being with what we are seeing,
receiving messages from, approaching, appropriating, is com-
munion. A practical necessity, the poem's process, which at
least momentarily fulfills want and wonder. And then you go
on, if you are luckily alert, to read or write the next poem . . .
and on . . . and on.

Somewhere in a previous Notebook I found that I had written the following . . .

What can we do to remind people in and out of school of the festivity in poetry? to perform its vitality? Make a fanfare of poetry, make a play of poems, make a holiday of Recitations. Poetry is grand opera about the most private and about the most public and cosmic, to think of it simply as a private prayer or a school subject is to repress its grandeur, to ignore its Festival nature. Exaltation is the basis of art as it is not of commentary.

Some Romantic poets give the impression that it's unromantic going to school, unromantic studying. That depends on many things—mostly the spiritual momentousness of the student. Lion hunting can really be dull; being a teacher or a student can really be bohemian, can be adventurous. Not on schedule and at will simply. To really meet a new book or a new person can sort of "change your life." It can be wonderful. The gods and the Muses can't be kept out of school; it's understandable why at times they won't go there. But it's wrong to think that great adventures can't happen there on the high seas. On the high C's of a prima donna. Poetry is a very surprising ocean; commentary is always bound to be a little mild; we can't even see all of the galaxies—or all of the students in one college; that's not tragic.

Poetry helps us remember what's brave and beautiful and sensible; to forget it is to have the life go out of us, the festival leave the community. It guards our sensibility.

School and poetry are meant for surprises. An acquaintance of mine, a very surprising poet—Jose Garcia Villa—said: "Education's only the envelope. Give me the Letter." When you really hear or read the poem you're receiving and sending great news. That's more than just "good" news. Also I like what Paul Valery said: "A poem is a holiday of Mind . . . Holiday: it is a game, but solemn, ordered and significant . . . One celebrates something in accomplishing it, or representing it in its purest form."   —J.T.

Robert Wallace:
IN ONE PLACE

             —something
holds up two or three leaves
the first year,

             and climbs
and branches, summer
by summer,

             till birds
in it don't remember
it wasn't there.

John Updike:
SEAGULLS

A gull, up close,
looks surprisingly stuffed.
His fluffy chest seems filled
with an inexpensive taxidermist's material
rather lumpily inserted. The legs,
unbent, are childish crayon strokes—
too simple to be workable.
And even the feather-markings,
whose intricate symmetry is the usual glory of birds,
are in the gull slovenly,
as if God makes too many
to make them very well.

Are they intelligent?
We imagine so, because they are ugly.
The sardonic one-eyed profile, slightly cross,
the narrow, ectomorphic head, badly combed,
the wide and nervous and well-muscled rump
all suggest deskwork: shipping rates
by day, Schopenhauer
by night, and endless coffee.

At that hour on the beach
when the flies begin biting in the renewed coolness
and the backsliding skin of the after-surf
reflects a pink shimmer before being blotted,
the gulls stand around in the dimpled sand
like those melancholy European crowds
that gather in cobbled public squares in the wake
of assassinations and invasions,
heads cocked to hear the latest radio reports.

It is also this hour when plump young couples
walk down to the water, bumping together,
and stand thigh-deep in the rhythmic glass.
Then they walk back toward the car,
tugging as if at a secret between them,
but which neither quite knows;
walk capricious paths through the scattering gulls,
as in some mythologies
beautiful gods stroll unconcerned
among our mortal apprehensions.

⏎ Students often ask if a poet or writer must wait until he
is inspired. My answer is always No; but I do remember the
moment of inspiration for "Seagulls." I was lying on the beach
in Ipswich, Massachusetts, in the very late afternoon of a summer or early fall day in 1959. As the beach crowds thinned,
the seagulls moved closer, and as I lay on my side, observing
one, the first lines of this poem came to me. They came in such
a rush, and seemed so precious and perishable, that I jumped
up and found a piece of charred wood from a beachfire and
wrote these lines on another, flatter piece of wood. I carried
the chunk home, amid embarrassing stares, and here inspiration must have ebbed, for the manuscript of the poem reveals
many alterations, an entire discarded section devoted to the
amorous young couple, and a completion date of December 5. I
evidently waited for some time for the nice turn in the final
stanza, when the camera lifts and we see people like gods
walking above these little apprehensive citizens of gulldom.

The form is, the student will notice, unrhymed "free" verse;
but I wrote much light verse in regular meters in those days,
and the ghosts of rhyme and stanza in my ear helped press my
lines toward the crispness that must exist in poetry. The second stanza always gets a laugh when I read it aloud, but I was
not consciously intending to be funny when I wrote it, merely

exact. I, too, in those days, felt ugly because I was intelligent, and I was settling into my writer's profession well aware of my "wide and nervous and well-muscled rump." The subject, in short, leaped to my heart with unforced self-symbolic import. Also, I enjoyed beaches in those days, and was happy being on one at any hour. "Happiness," in the double sense that the word "felicity" also contains, must exist for a poem to spring into being and to ripen toward its close with the requisite surprisingness (to the reader) and (from the writer's point of view) firmness and inevitability.   —J.U.

Philip Booth:
HERON

In the copper marsh
I saw a stilted heron
wade the tidal wash

and I, who caught no fish,
thought the grass barren
and that jade inlet harsh

until the quick-billed splash
of the long-necked heron
fulfilled my hunter's wish.

Then in the rising rush
of those great wings, far on
I saw the herring flash

and drop. And the dash
of lesser wings in the barren
marsh flew through my flesh.

142

Marge Piercy:
GRACIOUS GOODNESS

On the beach where we had been idly
telling the shell coins
cat's paw, cross-barred Venus, china cockle,
we both saw at once
the sea bird fall to the sand
and flap grotesquely.
He had taken a great barbed hook
out through the cheek and fixed
in the big wing.
He was pinned to himself to die,
a royal tern with a black crest blown back
as if he flew in his own private wind.
He felt good in my hands, not fragile
but muscular and glossy and strong,
the beak that could have split my hand
opening only to cry
as we yanked on the barbs.
We borrowed a clippers, cut and drew out the hook.
Then the royal tern took off, wavering,
lurched twice,
then acrobat returned to his element, dipped,
zoomed, and sailed out to dive for a fish.
Virtue: what a sunrise in the belly.
Why is there nothing
I have ever done with anybody
that seems to me so obviously right?

Donald Hall:
THE HENYARD ROUND

1
From the dark yard by the sheep barn the cock crowed
to the sun's pale
spectral foreblossoming eastward in June,
crowed,
 and crowed
later each day through fall and winter, this grand
conquistador of January drifts,
this almost-useless vain strutter
with wild monomaniac eye, burnished swollen chest;
yellow feet serpent-scaled, and bloodred comb,
who mounted with a mighty flutter
his busy hens: Generalissimo Rooster
of nobody's army.
 When he was old we cut his head off
on the sheepyard choppingblock, watching his drummajor
prance, his last resplendant march . . .
As I saw him diminish, as we plucked each feathery badge,
cut off his legs, eviscerated him,
and boiled him three hours for our fricasse Sunday
dinner, I understood
How the Mighty are Fallen, and my great-uncle Luther,
who could remember the Civil War,
risen from rest after his morning's sermon, asked
God's blessing on our food.

2
At the depot in April, parcel post went cheep-cheep
in big rectangular cardboard boxes, each
trembling with fifty chicks. When we opened
the carton in the cool toolshed
fifty downed fluffers cheep-cheeping
rolled and teetered.

144

                    All summer it was my chore
to feed and water them.
Twice a day I emptied a fouled pan
and freshened it from the trough; twice a day
I trudged up hill to the grainshed, filled
sapbuckets at wooden tubs and poured
pale grain into v-shaped feeders, watching the greedy
fluster and shove.
                    One summer
I nursed a blind chick six weeks—pale yellow,
frail, tentative, meek,
who never ate except when I gapped space for her.
I watched her grow little by little,
but every day outpaced
by the healthy beaks that seized feed
and grew monstrous—and one morning
discovered her dead: meatless, incorrigible . . .

3
At summer's end the small roosters
departed by truck, squawking with reason. Pullets
moved to the henhouse and extruded each day
new eggs, harvested morning and night. Hens roosted
in darkness locked from skunk and fox,
and let out at dawn footed the brittle yard,
tilting on stiff legs to peck the corncob
clean, to gobble orange peels, carrot tops, even
the shells of yesterday's eggs. Hens labored
to fill eggboxes the eggman shipped
to Boston, and to provide our breakfast, gathered
at the square table.
                    When the eggmaking frenzy
ceased, with each in her own time set
for weeks as if setting itself made eggs,
each used-up diligent hen
danced on the packed soil of the henyard her final

145

headless jig, and boiled like the rooster
in her pale shape featherless as an egg,
                                    consumed—
like the blind chick; like Nannie
who died one summer at eighty-seven, childish,
deaf, unable to feed herself, demented . . .

෨෨ Maybe I should begin by denying authority. I don't think
that a poet, speaking about his own poems, speaks a final word.
One observes one's own things from a unique perspective, but
hardly an objective one! Probably writers have more reason to
be deceived, by what they read on their own page, than other
readers do. I do agree that writers' notions about their own
work have some interest—but I suggest that it may be the interest of self-deception.

I think I began "The Henyard Round" out of the sense that
there was a poem somewhere among the bits and pieces of old
memory centering on roosters and hens and baby chicks . . .
I have worked on the poem four years, so far, and have made
something like a hundred and fifty drafts of it . . . After the
first six months or so, I began to notice the shape of it, the
roundness—hence the final title, which is a pun. (Speaking of
puns, I had tried calling it "The Poultry Society," for a while
. . . I'm glad I stopped.)

As I worked the poem over, I concentrated considerably on
sound—at first the grandiose and martial music of the rooster,
later the squeak of the baby chicks . . . (Look at the number
of long e's in the middle part.) Finally I worked towards a
resolved music in the last part, not so obvious perhaps, maybe
better for being less obvious.

For a long time, the poem ended not with Nannie but with
Luther's death. When it was Luther returning at the end, the
poem seemed too pat, *too much* a round, *too much* the snake
eating its own tail. One morning last summer I realized (as I
think) that I could zig a little to the side, and make it not

Luther but Nannie, because after all Nannie is Luther, except that she is not—and we all dance to the same tune.   —D.H.

Maxine Kumin:
THE HERMIT WAKES TO BIRD SOUNDS

He startles awake. His eyes are full of white light.
In a minute the sun will ooze into the sky.
Meanwhile, all the machines of morning start up.

The typewriter bird is at it again.
Her style is full of endearing hesitations.
The words, when they come, do so in
the staccato rush of a deceitful loveletter.

The sewing machine bird returns to the doddering elm.
Like Penelope, she rips out yesterday's stitches
only to glide up and down, front and back
reentering the same needle holes.

The bird who presides at the wellhouse primes the pump.
Two gurgles, a pause, four squeaks of the handle
and time after time a promise of water
can be heard falling back in the pipe's throat.

Far off the logging birds saw into heartwood
with rusty blades, and the grouse cranks up
his eternally unstartable Model T
and the oilcan bird comes with his liquid pock pock

to attend to the flinty clanks of the disparate parts
and as the old bleached sun slips into position
slowly the teasing inept malfunctioning
one-of-a-kind machines fall silent.

W. D. Snodgrass:
OWLS
—for Camille

Wait; the great horned owls
Calling from the wood's edge; listen.
There: the dark male, low
And booming, tremoring the whole valley.
There: the female, resolving, answering
High and clear, restoring silence.
The chilly woods draw in
Their breath, slow, waiting, and now both
Sound out together, close to harmony.

These are the year's worst nights.
Ice glazed on the top boughs,
Old snow deep on the ground,
Snow in the red-tailed hawks'
Nests they take for their own.
Nothing crosses the crusted ground.
No squirrels, no rabbits, the mice gone,
No crow has young yet they can steal.
These nights the iron air clangs
Like the gates of a cell block, blank
And black as the inside of your chest.

Now, the great owls take
The air, the male's calls take
Depth on and resonance, they take
A rough nest, take their mate
And, opening out long wings, take
Flight, unguided and apart, to caliper
The blind synapse their voices cross
Over the dead white fields,
The dead black woods, where they take
Soundings on nothing fast, take
Soundings on each other, each alone.

I suppose my weakness for owls began that first night when my former wife and I were moving into an old farmhouse near Erieville, N.Y. We were still carrying in boxes when a Great Horned Owl spoke, loud and clear, from the dark woods which we had imagined were ours. Its nest, we later found, was near the edge of those woods—when the leaves were down, we could see it from our kitchen window. For years, we never saw the owls. In the colder months each year, though, night after night, we heard them going out to hunt together about eleven o'clock, then coming back around four or five. During their mating season—the dead cold of January or February—the male's voice becomes incredibly resonant. Though smaller and less aggressive, he always speaks first; she answers him about a fifth higher. Gradually, the calls come closer together until you get a sort of harmony or counterpoint. It is very beautiful—if you don't happen to be a squirrel or rabbit.

Then, in our ninth or tenth year there, quite suddenly the female became visible, peering up over the edge of her nest or, if we came too close, diving down to soar off through the woods. She looked like a St. Bernard with awnings.

That same year, in a sharp storm, her nest came down; for several weeks, we were raising owlets—two balls of under-bed fnuff grown to the size of hornets' nests. In the center of each were two big, yellowy eyes and a beak that clacked menacingly until you gave the owls' call; then the fluffballs clucked contentedly and cuddled up to feed or sleep. After our local bird expert discovered the parent birds still in the area, we built a new nest and hauled the babies up where their real parents could safely tend them, but where we could watch. And, I confess, we climbed ladders every afternoon to feed them, too.

The next year our expert turned up an orphan for us. I spent months cruising the back roads, looking for road kills—small animals or birds that had been hit and could now be hauled home, chopped up, then frozen and fed, bit by bit, to my hungry fluffball. When she was large enough to fly, we shut her in a cabin nearby where she could strengthen her wings but would not fly off before we had taught her to hunt. Several times each day I went in with her to drag her food in front of her on a string; later, I made her take it always on the wing. I doubt that I have ever done anything more strange.

All this probably suggests *why* I should write about owls; how is another matter. During that same time I had been experimenting with a rhythmic technique I had first found in Walt Whitman, our first and greatest free verse poet. A number of his finest poems begin by stating a rhythmic theme, then develop and sophisticate that theme, much like a set of musical theme and variations. In his Civil War book, *Drum Taps,* for instance, is a fine short piece, "Cavalry Crossing a Ford" which begins

Ă líne iň lóng ărráy,‖whеře thĕy wínd bĕtwíxt gréĕn íslănds,/ . . .

Here the theme is a unit of three beats, given (as so frequently) twice in the first line. Yet, even here the second unit has two more unaccented syllables and an extra half-stress ("green") between the main accents. The next line gives further variants, lengthening the line to three such units, a process of variations which continues through the poem. Or one may trace a similar process in the very next poem, "Bivouac on a Mountain Side," which starts, again, with two units of three beats each:

Ĭ sée bĕfоře mĕ nów‖ă trávelliňg ármў háltĭng,/ . . .

No doubt, though, the most famous and powerful use of such a device by Whitman is in the opening of what I think the finest lyric written in America:

Oút of the crádlĕ,‖eńdlĕsslў róckiňg,/ . . .

In so long and powerful a poem, of course, this is not the only rhythmic or metric device. Still, the use of this rhythm to propel and control the first long verse paragraph, then its uncanny return at the end of the poem, seem strokes of the sheerest genius. And it is worth nothing that neither effect was present in his first published version; both had to be found through patient years of experiment and revision.

For my own poem, I took for my theme-rhythm the call of the Great Horned Owl:

HOÓ, hŏo-HÓO, HÓO, HÓO.

My first line reproduces that rhythm closely:

Waít, thĕ Great Horned Owls,/

The second line adds to this basic four-beat rhythm several unaccented syllables:

Cálliñg frŏm thĕ woóds' edge, lístĕn./

The third drops the extra syllable, repeating the basic pattern:

Thére: thĕ dark mále, lów/

but immediately rushes into the fourth line where many more unaccented syllables are added:

Añd bóominğ, trĕmŏriñg thĕ whóle vállĕy./

And so on throughout the poem; when such a technique works well, I think it will seem not only a restraint, a limit on the poem's energies, but will come to be identified with that energy itself, an energy which is only strengthened by being restrained and channelled.

Naturally, I don't expect readers to know of this theme-and-variations structure, much less know that this theme is the rhythm of the owl's call. We don't usually ask about the principles of construction in a building we like; we just use it that much more. Now I must abide the test of seeing how many people will want to inhabit and use my structure and for how long.   —W.D.S.

Richard Shelton:
REQUIEM FOR SONORA

1
a small child of a wind
stumbles toward me down the arroyo
lost and carrying no light
tearing its sleeves
on thorns of the palo verde
talking to itself
and to the dark shapes it touches
searching for what it has not lost
and will never find
searching
and lonelier
than even I can imagine

the moon sleeps
with her head on the buttocks of a young hill
and you lie before me
under moonlight as if under water
oh my desert
the coolness of your face

2
men are coming inland to you
soon they will make you the last resort
for tourists who have
nowhere else to go

what will become of the coyote
with eyes of topaz
moving silently to his undoing
the ocotillo

flagellant of the wind
the deer climbing with dignity
further into the mountains
the huge and delicate saguaro
what will become of those who cannot learn
the terrible knowledge of cities

3
years ago I came to you as a stranger
and have never been worthy
to be called your lover or to speak your name
loveliest
most silent sanctuary
mòre fragile than forests
more beautiful than water

I am older and uglier
and full of the knowledge
that I do not belong to beauty
and beauty does not belong to me
I have learned to accept
whatever men choose to give me
or whatever they choose to withhold
but oh my desert
yours is the only death I cannot bear

༄ The poem was written after I had lived in the Sonora
Desert in Southern Arizona about fifteen years. During that
time I had seen the accelerating encroachment on the desert
and its wildlife by agriculture and urban development. As more
and more people came to the Southwest, huge tracts of the
desert were bulldozed—no living thing was left standing—in
order to build thousands of acres of houses. In other places the
lush desert growth was leveled in order to plant cotton and

other crops. All of this "progress" has seriously depleted the water table.

A desert, like tundra, is a very delicate landscape. When its plants are destroyed, serious erosion occurs, and the growth cannot restore itself. Several deserts on this continent have been completely destroyed. The Colorado Desert in Southwestern California does not even occur on the map today. Until the 1920's it was one of the most beautiful deserts in the world.

After years of frustrated efforts to impede "progress" in the desert, I wrote "Requiem for Sonora" very quickly one night. It required little revision, unlike most of my poems. In the process of writing it, I came to realize what I had been unable to face earlier: the desert was dying and there was nothing I could do to keep it alive. Realizing that, I gave the poem its title. A requiem is a song for the dead. Writing the poem was a process of discovery for me—discovering something I knew but did not know I knew. I hope it will provide a similar process for the reader.   —R.S.

Mark Vinz:
WILD WEST

Trouble is, it's getting harder
and harder to find a good horse—
even the stage to Tombstone is a
Chevrolet. Posses and Indians
will only work for union scale,
the cavalry is fighting hostiles
on the far side of the moon.

Good whiskey must be part of
someone else's dream—most folks
in this town roll funny cigarettes.

154

You ever hear of dancehall girls
in pantsuits? A schoolmarm
teaching sex education classes?
Wagon trains don't stop here anymore.
No squaredances in years.

On the other hand, the mayor's still
the sneaky little dude who owns most of
the ranches and the only good hotel.
You don't have to travel far to find
a poisoned well. Snake-oil shows and
lynchings happen almost every day.
There's always a gunslinger or two
ready to prove who packs the biggest gun—
out here along the windy Interstates,
where our shadows stretch for miles.

John Updike:
TELEPHONE POLES

They have been with us a long time.
They will outlast the elms.
Our eyes, like the eyes of a savage sieving the trees
In his search for game,
Run through them. They blend along small-town streets
Like a race of giants that have faded into mere mythology.
Our eyes, washed clean of belief,
Lift incredulous to their fearsome crowns of bolts, trusses,
        struts, nuts, insulators, and such
Barnacles as compose
These weathered encrustations of electrical debris—
Each a Gorgon's head, which, seized right,
Could stun us to stone.

Yet they are ours. We made them.
See here, where the cleats of linemen
Have roughened a second bark
Onto the bald trunk. And these spikes
Have been driven sideways at intervals handy for human legs.
The Nature of our construction is in every way
A better fit than the Nature it displaces.
What other tree can you climb where the birds' twitter,
Unscrambled, is English? True, their thin shade is negligible,
But then again there is not that tragic autumnal
Casting-off of leaves to outface annually.
These giants are more constant than evergreens
By being never green.

Ed Ochester:
THE GIFT

One day
as I was lying on the lawn
dreaming of the Beautiful
and my wife was justifiably bitching
   out the window
at my shiftlessness and
the baby was screaming
because I wouldn't let him
eat my cigarettes,
a tiger cat leaped over the fence,
smiled at my wife,
let the baby pull his tail,
hummed like a furry dynamo
as I stroked him.

My wife took the car to get him some food,
my son began to sing his wordless song,
and I wrote a poem in the sand.

Now God give every man who's hopeless
a beautiful wife,
an infant son who sings,
and the gift of a sweet-faced cat.

⇗ Most poems aren't directly and fully autobiographical, and the reasons for that are fairly simple. For one thing, if I tried to describe *every* thing I did or thought about in a period of time, most of it would be inconsequential and dull ("I breathed in and out/ and scratched my left ear/ and breathed in and out/ and ate a peanut butter sandwich/ on Smorg's white bread"—who cares?); writers pick and choose what seem to be the most important parts of their experience. For another thing, poets like novelists often choose to write about experiences that haven't actually happened to them. Many of the people I've met—miners, farmworkers, a publishing tycoon, two convicted murderers, a jazz musician, and others—have had very interesting lives quite different from my own, and sometimes I want to tell their stories, or speak in their voices, and if I'm lucky enough to write a poem about them that seems authentic and moving to someone, that reader shouldn't make the mistake of thinking that the poem is necessarily autobiographical.

But "The Gift" is autobiographical. It "really happened" in Gainesville, Florida, when I was teaching at the university there shortly after our son Ned was born. I was doing, as I've always done, a lot of daydreaming then—I guess that's supposed to be the writer's occupational disease, but that's the time we're really working, planning things out, getting the words together—and on that day things weren't working out very well. I was thinking about some project while I was supposed to be taking care of Ned, but—obviously—not paying much attention to him. And it was the middle of the summer, so hot in Florida that even the banana trees were sagging. The heat probably had something to do with my wife Britt's exasperation with me: "if you can't even watch the baby, for goodness' sake. . . ." And that's when the tiger cat leapt over the fence.

What struck me as important, and the reason I wanted to get it into a poem, is that so much of our lives is like this. What turns out to be important is what you hadn't expected and couldn't have planned on, and that very often in itself seems inconsequential. You get up in the morning and there's a wren singing outside your window and it puts you in a good mood for the rest of the day. You go into a restaurant and there's something suspicious and crunchy in your spaghetti and suddenly your good mood is ruined. Or a cat jumps over the fence and, if you like animals, you forget your own troubles for a while. Everybody knows, even if we don't want to believe it, how important chance is in our lives. "The Gift" is about chance and, I suppose, about hope: if we don't take ourselves too seriously, not all the time anyway, casual events may enrich or change our lives. The three people in "The Gift" are momentarily silly because they're so much locked into their private patterns that they forget for the moment that they love one another. The animal is the catalyst—who would have predicted it?—that gets them past a bad time.

"The Gift" is one of the most popular poems I've ever written. Whenever I do it at a poetry reading people come up to say how much they like it, and I think that what they mean is that the poem is realistically optimistic, "true" to their own experience even if they couldn't have verbalized it before. We're all "hopeless" in some way or another, and if we're intelligent we know it, but we also ought to know that if we stay loose and open to experience we'll get past that knowledge.

Anyway, the poem got written that night in a couple of minutes, one of the fastest poems I've ever done. I changed one word four or five years later: originally my son was singing his "little wordless song" and I decided that the word *little* connoted a kind of cuteness that I thought was damaging and misleading, so I dropped it. And the cat? The cat kept coming around for a while. We fed it, and it would leave us an occasional gift of a dead squirrel on the front porch. You may not like dead squirrels yourself—I don't—but you have to stay loose about these things. That's the best gift that a cat, certainly a free cat, can give so far as a cat knows. We never had a real name for him; we called him "Cat," and he disappeared shortly before we left Florida to move to Pennsylvania. We hoped he was o.k., and that he had moved on for inscrutable cat reasons to other people who needed him.   —E.O.

159

Marvin Bell:
WHAT THEY DO TO YOU IN DISTANT PLACES

I never told you.
There was a woman—in the greening season
of a tropical island
where I had gone to break some hard thoughts
across my knee
and also, although I am no athlete
but breathe with my stomach like the satyr
and live in my stomach
according to bile and acid and bread and bitter chocolate,
to run a long race for the first time.
On that morning,
it was raining in great screens
of the purest water and almost no one at 4 a.m.
where I waited, half-sheltered
by the edge of my dark hotel, for a let-up.
Except her, suddenly
from nowhere—smelling of long hair and dew,
smelling of dew and grass and a little powder.
She wore a dress that moved.
She had been out dancing and the night and she
were young.
I wore a black watch cap like an old sailor
but I was all there was.

I said no, I had to do something else.
She asked how far? And
if I would run all that way—hours.
I said I'd try,
and then she kissed me for luck
and her mouth on mine was as sweet as the wild guava
and the smell of her hair
was that of the little bit of dew the lover

brings home from the park
when again she shows up in the morning.

I don't know where I have been
that I have ever had such a kiss
that asked nothing and gave everything.
I walked out into the rain
as if blessed. But I had forgotten
what they do to you in distant places,
taking away your memory
before sending you back. You and me.
I confess,
I forgot her within the hour
in the gross odors of my labors.
If I had known what she was doing. . . .
Perhaps she's with you now.

In March of 1978, I decided to run the Honolulu Marathon that December. I was thirty pounds overweight and forty-one years old, and I had not run a mile at one time ever in my life. In high school I had played soccer and basketball, and in the Police Athletic League I had played baseball, and, while I had had my small successes as an athlete in a small town on Long Island, even there I was no star.

I was my only coach and stupidly built up my mileage too quickly. By June, I was running 12–13 miles at a time on hills. I suffered injuries, came back from them, suffered others and finally ruined my chances by continuing to run long distances with a knee injury received, not from running, but from running into a bookcase at work! Honolulu would have to wait until 1979.

By the time I arrived in Hawaii, ten days before the 1979 Marathon, I was injured again. I had been able to muster only minimal mileage for running a marathon, about 45 miles a week. I had an ache in one leg. I had trained in the winter of Iowa, wearing extra clothes to imitate the effect of Hawaii's heat, but Hawaii was hotter and more humid than I had anticipated. I couldn't stretch during that last week, or run, for fear of aggravating my injury. By race day, I had no idea whether I would be able to run a mile, or ten, or the whole 26 miles, 385 yards.

I wanted to do it, desperately. I had made it a personal challenge. It wouldn't mean much to anyone else, but it would mean a lot to me. I ate badly in Hawaii, I couldn't sleep the night before. Finally, I came down to the lobby of my hotel at four a.m. to walk to Kapiolani Park to take a bus to the starting line at the Aloha Tower. Race time would be six-thirty a.m. I wore a black wool sailor's cap, as I always do in cold or rain, and a warm-up suit against the chill, and I carried in a satchel all sorts of things I wouldn't need.

What I needed was a "shot in the arm," some encouragement, some mystical inspiration perhaps. Which is what I got— from a stranger in the rain. The story of that stranger is told in "What They Do to You in Distant Places."

We all need that sort of encouragement from time to time: not advice, not an iron-clad promise, not a lie intended to pump us up, but simply the kind of support that doesn't depend on victory but says good luck and means it.

The race took place as scheduled on the hottest day in the history of the Honolulu Marathon. I finished it, not without doubt and pain. I hurt enough afterwards that I didn't think again of that girl in the rain for weeks.

Who was she? What was she? She was free of me, wherever and whoever she was, free to work her magic on someone else who needs it at that moment. And if not her, then someone else. Perhaps she's with you now . . .

Memory is partial, selective, vague. We can't recapture the full sense of what it was like to be alive in a certain place at a particular moment simply by remembering. That's another thing they do to you in distant places—"taking away your memory before sending you back."

The poem brings back more of the moment, as well as some second thoughts and an idea about it (perhaps she's with you now). When the tiny proof print of me crossing the finish line arrived, my wife said, "Oh, look, you're smiling." "I'm not smiling," I countered. "Oh, look," she said, "You're smiling." "I'm not smiling," I said. When the enlargement came, she looked and said, "You're not smiling."

The poem is mostly about the smiling part.   —*M.B.*

William Dickey:
THE FISH UPSTAIRS

You tell me over the telephone about your world.
The world that you inhabit has no color
because you are miserable, deserted by the one you love.
If you have no color, nothing will be allowed color.
Your flat sand landscape permits even itself no end.

And at the same time, as you anticipate
remaining miserable, your mind teases itself
with the idea of a hummingbird outside the window.
Quickly, the hummingbird is made destitute.
It has neither food nor friends nor a reason for being.
It must be an incredibly stupid bird. Yet it seems real.

Thus the world, that does not want to be
rejected by you, edges itself back in
around the corner of a door, gives you a hamburger
it hopes you can taste, sends in a little breeze
to make you realize that the back of your neck is naked.
It tries to retrieve you from wherever you have been mislaid.

The world has enough images so that it hopes to win.
It has the lime trees on the patio, the fish upstairs.
Whatever room misery walks into, it finds an image.
Not wanting to, it accepts the image into itself.
Itself becomes different, containing a hummingbird.

I do not need, over the telephone, to give you
the good advice you ask for; the advice is there.
The city hovers, redthroat, outside your window,
telling you how you are yourself, how you are many.
Now you will go and look at the fish upstairs.

Richard Eberhart:
ON A SQUIRREL CROSSING THE ROAD IN AUTUMN, IN NEW ENGLAND

It is what he does not know,
Crossing the road under the elm trees,
About the mechanism of my car,
About the Commonwealth of Massachusetts,
About Mozart, India, Arcturus,

That wins my praise. I engage
At once in whirling squirrel-praise.

He obeys the orders of nature
Without knowing them.
It is what he does not know
That makes him beautiful.
Such a knot of little purposeful nature!

I who can see him as he cannot see himself
Repose in the ignorance that is his blessing.

It is what man does not know of God
Composes the visible poem of the world.
. . . Just missed him!

✍ This poem was caused by the event it describes. I realized
that I had not hit the squirrel. The poem explains my thoughts
and feelings about this experience.   —R.E.

William Dickey:
HAPPINESS

I sent you this bluebird of the name of Joe
with "Happiness" tattooed onto his left bicep.
(For a bluebird, he was a damn good size.)
And all you can say is you think your cat has got him?

I tell you the messages aren't getting through.
The Golden Gate Bridge is up past its ass in traffic;
tankers colliding, singing telegrams out on strike.
The machineries of the world are raised in anger.

So I am sending this snail of the name of Fred
in a small tricolor sash, so the cat will know him.
He will scrawl out "Happiness" in his own slow way.
I won't ever stop until the word gets to you.

✍ This poem and "The Fish Upstairs" come out of the
everyday world of bills, the morning mail, a museum visit, a
telephone conversation. Their intention is to look at that world
as closely as possible, to look at it as it is, not as we have been
taught to expect it to be. The world *is* unexpected, if it is given

a chance; it is full of surprises. A poet is someone who will not give up the ability to be surprised, and so he is both excited by what he sees, and never safe.   —W.D.

John Tagliabue:
I SOUGHT ALL OVER THE WORLD

I sought all over the world for a present for you until I found
    the sky
And in it was the world and you and me. I was there with
    my love bright as the sun
You were there with your love moony as the night, dark, and
    pearls were everywhere for lovers,
The children climbed the trees on that bright and light day.
    I looked all over the world
For a present for you and then I made you see yourself
    and me in creation
In God and then I was, we were, very happy. The children
    laughed in the tree.

Marvin Bell:
TO DOROTHY

You are not beautiful, exactly.
You are beautiful, inexactly.
You let a weed grow by the mulberry
and a mulberry grow by the house.
So close, in the personal quiet
of a windy night, it brushes the wall
and sweeps away the day till we sleep.

A child said it, and it seemed true:
"Things that are lost are all equal."
But it isn't true. If I lost you,
the air wouldn't move, nor the tree grow.
Someone would pull the weed, my flower.
The quiet wouldn't be yours. If I lost you,
I'd have to ask the grass to let me sleep.

X. J. Kennedy:
TO DOROTHY ON HER EXCLUSION FROM
THE *GUINNESS BOOK OF WORLD RECORDS*

Not being Breedlove, whose immortal skid
Bore him for six charmed miles on screeching brakes;
Not having whacked from Mieres to Madrid
The longest-running hoop; at ducks and drakes
The type whose stone drowns in a couple of skips
Even if pitty-pats be counted plinkers;
Smashing of face, but having launched no ships;
Not of a kidney with beer's foremost drinkers;

Fewer the namesakes that display your brand
Than Prout has little protons—yet you win
The world with just a peerless laugh. I stand
Stricken amazed: you merely settle chin
Into a casual fixture of your hand
And a uniqueness is, that hasn't been.

〰 If you've ever browsed in the *Guinness Book,* that fasci-
nating collection of incredible records (some of them pretty
silly), you may have met some of the records mentioned in this
poem. Craig Breedlove, named in the first line, was tooling his
jet-propelled racing car along the Bonneville Salt Flats in Utah
one day, when his brakes locked. The result was that his car
made the longest skid marks ever measured. Another record I
love: there's a Spanish hoop-roller who once rolled his hoop
nearly two hundred miles. Next, the poem refers to those serious players of ducks and drakes who hold a yearly conven-
tion, where they try to skip flat stones across a pool for as
many times as possible. In line ten, who is Prout? He was a
nineteenth-century physicist who claimed to have given his
name to the proton, the atomic particle. This may not be a
real world's record: I believe the word *proton* comes from
Greek. But if we honor Prout's claim, then no other person
has more things in the universe named after him.

Knowing these trivial facts may help you make sense out of
the poem—I hope! I wrote it out of my long fondness for the
Guinness Book and for my wife Dorothy. As you can gather
from the poem, Dorothy isn't the kind of person who sets daz-
zling records. Yet it seemed to me that, in her own way, she is
unique. This poem is an attempt to say how.

There is nothing unique, though, in the poem's shape and
pattern. It is a sonnet: a poem of fourteen lines that follows a
certain scheme of rhymes. For more than six centuries, poets
have been churning out this type of thing. Nowadays, some
think that the sonnet form is played out from overuse. (My

friend Robert Bly says, "Sonnets are where old professors go to die.") Still, I enjoy the difficulties of the sonnet—and the challenge of trying to do something a little bit new in such an old form.

What grabs me about the sonnet (and about all demanding forms) is the serious game you have to play in writing such poetry. Working in rhyme, you don't absolutely control the direction your poem is heading in. At times, you yearn to say something, but the infernal rhymes won't let you. They keep suggesting odd new possibilities far from your mind. You're like someone crossing a river on stepping-stones, obliged to walk where the stones permit. You struggle to keep your balance, while at the same time trying to go where you want to go. Often, in writing a rhyming poem, you end up somewhere you didn't expect.

To me, this sort of writing crackles with thrills and surprises. Of course, most of my efforts to get the rhymes to come out right fail miserably. If you write in rhyme, you have to keep dumping your wastebasket. Sometimes, to save paper, I compose mentally. I wrote a rough draft of "To Dorothy . . ." in my head.   —X.J.K.

Richard Wilbur:
APOLOGY

A word sticks in the wind's throat;
A wind-launch drifts in the swells of rye;
Sometimes, in broad silence,
The hanging apples distil their darkness.

You, in a green dress, calling, and with brown hair,
Who come by the field-path now, whose name I say
Softly, forgive me love if also I call you
Wind's word, apple-heart, haven of grasses.

Gary Gildner:
LETTER TO A SUBSTITUTE TEACHER

Dear Miss Miller,
You are someone
too sweet to sleep alone
and I can't help myself

sitting here hearing
your soft voice so
I must tell you
I like you

very much and would like
to know you better.
I know there is a difference
in our age and race

but we do have something
in common—You're a girl
and I'm a boy
and that is all

we need. Please
do not look at me
like I'm silly or sick
and most of all

please do not reject
my very first love
affair. If you do
not feel the same

as I do please
tell me how I can forget
your unforgettable voice
that reminds me

of Larry the Duke's pet
birds in the morning,
your blue eyes like the
Blessed Virgin's,

your golden hair and your
nice red mouth. Please
give me some sign
of how you feel,

I would rather be hurt
than forgotten forever.
Sincerely yours,
The Boy in the Green Shirt.

Howard Moss:
AT THE ALGONQUIN

He sat at the Algonquin, smoking a cigar.
A coffin of a clock bonged out the time.
She was ten minutes late. But in that time,
He puffed the blue eternity of his cigar.

Did she love him still? His youth was gone.
Humiliation's toad, with its blank stares
Squatted on his conscience. When they went upstairs,
Some version of them both would soon be gone.

Before that, though, drinks, dinner, and a play—
The whole demanding, dull expense account.
You paid these days for things of no account.
Whatever love may be, it's not child's play.

Slowly she walked toward him. God, we are
Unnatural animals! The scent of roses
Filled the room above the carpet's roses,
And, getting up, he said, "Ah, *there* you are!"

◌ The "Algonquin" refers to a well-known, small, and dis-
tinguished hotel in New York City on West 44th Street. (The
word "Algonquin," in turn, refers to a tribe of Indians, though
the poem makes no use of that meaning of the word.) The
hotel was the home of the "Algonquin Round Table," a liter-
ary-journalistic-gossip group famed for its alleged wit and
worldliness in the 1920's, and more fabled in memory than in
fact—almost all of the anecdotes associated with it are rather
tepid. What makes the hotel truly memorable is a lobby that
looks like a large, old-fashioned living-room with deep chairs
and couches and tables where people come to drink, pass the
time, and chat. Walking into the room seems like walking into
another world far different from the hurly-burly of the street
outside. The atmosphere of another era is carefully preserved.
Someone was foresighted and cunning enough to see that pre-
serving the old would someday be worth more than replacing
it with the new. That has proved to be the case: The Algonquin's unique interior is its most valuable possession. Because
the hotel is opposite the office I work in, I have gone there
fairly frequently over the years and have sat in the poem's
room, waiting (especially before the hotel became too famous
and crowded) for someone to arrive. "At the Algonquin" is an
"observed" poem in that I actually saw the incident it describes, though I added made-up, dramatic possibilities to a

small incident. As for the details, they, too, are real: there is a grandfather clock that chimes the hours (see stanza one) and a carpet patterned with roses (see stanza four). The cigar, though, may have been a pipe—I'm not sure. This poem has a rhyme scheme I call a "sandwich" rhyme: there are two rhyme words in each stanza—each the same as the word it rhymes with— and the first and the fourth lines enclose the middle couplet of lines two and three. The technical point of the poem was to use a very strict rhyme scheme while keeping the tone conversational and natural. —*H.M.*

Robert Wallace:
THE GIRL WRITING HER ENGLISH PAPER

lies on one hip by the fire,
blond, in jeans.

The wreckage of her labor, elegant as Eden
or petals from a tree,
surrounds her—

a little farm, smoke rising from the ashtray,
book, notebooks, papers, fields;
a poem's furrows.

If the lights were to go out suddenly,
stars would be overhead,
their light come in.

ℯ "The Girl Writing Her English Paper" grew out of watching a girlfriend, once upon a time, sprawled before a fireplace working on a course paper about a poem. Her concentration was complete, and the clutter of her book, notebooks, papers, and ashtray made a little scene from which, though I was in the room, I felt excluded. Outside, I recall, it was a cold and snowy evening, and wind blustered around the eaves of the old house.

The girl's absorption both made her very beautiful to me and seemed to make the outer world irrelevant. What she was doing—attending carefully to the words of a man long dead, although her real lover was nearby—piqued my jealousy. It seemed to say something, too, about the power of poetry.

Looking back, I see that the images tell a good deal about my feelings. The images just "came," I didn't "think them up"—and so they have a psychological complexity I didn't consciously intend. Both Eden and the spring image of petals fallen from a tree suggest the girl's beauty, and Eden may also suggest, in recalling Adam and Eve, how close I felt to her. But the petals are scattered and fallen. So the image also has overtones of the fragility of beauty and the wreckage time brings to everything. Eden, too, evokes negative connotations—the sinful fall of humankind, the end of paradise, and God's curse that they should thereafter earn their living by the sweat of their brow. The girl's writing her paper is also a "labor," a cost. (No doubt I was remembering Yeats' wonderful poem "Adam's Curse" in which a beautiful woman says, " 'To be born woman is to know— / Although they do not talk of it at school— / That we must labour to be beautiful.' ")

Yet the scene in stanza three—the "little farm"—is at once an image of labor and of a happy, natural life. The "smoke rising from the ashtray" signals warmth and comfort. The likeness of papers and fields—both rectangular, with lines or rows—connects the poem with this productive activity. I was thinking as well of our word *verse,* which comes from the Latin verb *verso-versare,* meaning "to turn." (It shows up in such other words as *reverse,* "to turn back.") The past participle *versus* originally meant "having turned" and so came to be the noun first for furrows—the turning of the plow—and then for any rows or lines. Hence, the "poem's furrows."

Stanza four insists on the reality of the girl's labor and beauty. So natural is it all, I felt, that the permanent and lovely stars would affirm both the labor and the beauty. And, indeed, though unseen, the stars were in fact shining up there beyond the snow clouds and the wind.

"The Girl Writing Her English Paper" is a poem I treasure for what it made me see about my own complicated feelings and about the pleasures and sadnesses of life. I know it is a good poem, not because of any craft or technical skill it may show, but because it was able to surprise me with how much more I knew than I knew I knew. The story has an ending the poem would probably understand. Later, the girl and I were married; and later, divorced.   —R.W.

Mark Vinz:
NOVEMBER SONG

Tonight, the first snow:
the starless dark we
wrap our coats around,
clinging to autumn
like the last dry leaf.

The wind is a stalker
rattling all our doors,
the wind is a beggar
wanting only to be loved.

A long fast freight
tunnels through town—
Montana coal train
riding its black message
from the west,
ringed in frost and smoke.
In each small fire
there is a tiny song of sleep.

Tonight, the first snow dreams:
the wind is an old beggar
rattling our bones in his cup.

Howard Nemerov:
THE DYING GARDEN

The flowers get a darkening brilliance now,
And in the still sun-heated air stand out
As stars and soloists where they had been before
Choruses and choirs; at the equinox,

I mean, when the great gyroscope begins
To spin the sun under the line and do
Harvest together with fall: the time that trees
Crimp in their steepled shapes, the hand of leaf
Become a claw; when wealth and death are one,
When moth and wasp and mouse come in the house
For comfort if they can; the deepening time
When sketchy Orion begins his slow cartwheel
About the southern sky, the time of turn
When moth and wasp and mouse come in the house
To die there as they may; and there will be,
You know, All Saints, All Souls, and Halloween,
The killing frost, the end of Daylight Time,
Sudden the nightfall on the afternoon
And on children scuffling home through drifts of leaf;
Till you drop the pumpkins on the compost heap,
The blackened jack o'lanterns with their candled eyes,
And in the darkening garden turn for home
Through summer's flowers now all gone, withdrawn,
The four o'clocks, the phlox, the hollyhocks,
Somber November in amber and umber embering out.

❧ The genesis of my own compositions does not as a rule
much occupy my mind; while writing, one is too busy to think
about it, beyond the fleeting notion that it is after all remarkable that one thing should follow another as if ordained to do
so and without conscious attention on the writer's part. And
afterwards it is too late, for the poem has replaced its thoughts,
if indeed these had a separate existence at all. Lu Chi says in
his Wen Fu, or prose poem on the art of poetry, that the poet's
work is "to follow the skein of the seasons, with a sigh at their
passing," and I am satisfied with that. But here is the little I
can remember.

The title belongs to my wife, as indeed the garden does itself. The moment of the poem, its occasion, seems to me among

the most poignant of the year, equalled only by the first snow, and, less dramatically, by the first feeling of the sun's warmth in spring.

Some of the details had been in my mind for years, "the hand of leaf/ Become a claw" is one such; others are "When moth and wasp and mouse come in the house/ For comfort if they can," and "The four o'clocks, the phlox, the hollyhocks," a series I said over to myself, varying the order all ways, many times at that time of year. And I had long been taken by the coming more or less together of all those holidays concerned with death and the first real frost and the end of Daylight Saving with its magical and decisive shifting of the sun back over fifteen degrees of arc in an instant, placing the darkness into late afternoon again instead of morning.

As for the repetition with variation of the bit about moth and wasp and mouse, it got in there by the happiest inadvertency; while copying a draft of the piece, my attention slipped, or I looked up and out the window, and when I got back to the page I started as if several lines above where I really was. When I noticed the error I was very pleased with it, and so it stayed.

Some reviews I've just got from the publisher of *Sentences* (the collection in which the poem first appeared) take particular and jeering exception to the poem's last line. One reviewer says "The line not only attempts to out-Hopkins Hopkins," which was news to me, "but topples over into nonsense verse," which still is news to me. Another said it was "a final image that Tennyson at his silliest could not have expressed so ineptly," adding that "nothing in the poem suggests that this line should be taken as a joke."

Well, as Isaac Babel so marvelously said, a phrase is born into the world both good and bad at the same time. This phrase was born into the world at the fiftieth birthday of the high school I had attended as a boy. I was invited back for a day of classes, a reading, and so on, and while teaching one of these

I happened to look out the window over the pupils' heads at the somber rising landscape of rock and woods, and said to the class, quite without premeditation, "Isn't it amazing that language allows us to say things like "Somber November in amber and umber embering out? a compound of likeness and difference of sounds that still makes sense? Of course," I added, "you'd never do it, but all the same isn't it amazing," &c &c. And so, of course, when the phrase returned to mind a couple of years later, I did it. I'm a contrary fellow, especially to myself.

Neither reviewer, also of course, noticed that the line immediately preceding, the one about phlox and hollyhocks and four o'clocks, was doing something quite similar, so either aggravating the fault or making it into a method; nor did they appear to know that such effects are by no means foreign to their finest poetry, as for instance in Burns':

O who will mow me now, my Jo,
An' who will mow me now?
The sojer wi' his bandoliers
Has banged my belly fu'.

Which is from the less well-known version of "Comin' Through the Rye."

Reviewers to the contrary, some friends have liked the line. And I take comfort from the admonition to poets of W. H. Auden:

Be subtle, various, ornamental, clever,
And do not listen to those critics ever
Whose crude provincial gullets crave in books
Plain cooking made still plainer by plain cooks.
As though the Muse preferred her half-wit sons.

"The Truest Poetry is the Most Feigning," title straight out of the Forest of Arden.   —H.N.

179

William Carpenter:
AUTUMN
—*for Steve Katona*

This morning they are putting away the whales.
As always, it is a vast operation.
The long line of whales almost reaches the horizon.
The orderlies slide the whale-car on its old rails
into the sea, the men in boats coax the whales
into alignment with the car. They fasten on the ropes.
You can see how the whale has come to rest squarely
on the timbers. It is not made to be in the air;
without support the bones and sides would collapse.
It would die of its own weight.
They have done this year after year, in autumn,
and their fathers and grandfathers before them,
for there is no emigration from here, and they marry
mostly their own kind. I myself came from away,
but I see my own son in one of the small boats,
appeasing the whales, keeping them in the line
as they wait out the slow craft of being hauled,
as they abide their transit from the first waters
into the cold air. They are hauling the whales
and the whole town gathers before sunrise.
An abnormal tide laps at the road itself
as they open the doors to the whale-houses
and begin moving them in.
The breathing of dry whales is slow,
their vapor smells of the inside of the sea,
and the natives say on the day that they haul whales
you can feel heartbeats in the earth
even as you drive your car over the road.
Evening descends suddenly in the whale yard.
We are cleaning the last of them with wire brooms,
for the whale carries a whole civilization on its back,

mussels and crabs and grass. One of the boys
finds a small octopus and we jump back
as if he had shown us a death's head.
When the last whale is moved into its shed,
as far as we can see, the ocean is empty.
A small flight of geese crosses the surface;
nothing remains inside. We close the doors,
we begin banking foundations for the long winter.

Frank Steele:
MARKINGS

Along the cement walkway I pick up
a brown leaf, wet since October.
Beneath it is a perfect print
of a brown leaf, its splay
deckle rained in through stiff pores
like an engraving.

Fallen leaves that find true ground
have easy deaths, disappearing
into futures they can picture
all the way down. But the stopped leaf
stays, finds a way to say
how hard dying is.
                Thinking of this,
I find I have one leaf
to throw away
and one to keep.

William Jay Smith:
QUAIL IN AUTUMN

Autumn has turned the dark trees toward the hill;
The wind has ceased; the air is white and chill.
Red leaves no longer dance against your foot,
The branch reverts to tree, the tree to root.

And now in this bare place your step will find
A twig that snaps flintlike against the mind;
Then thundering above your giddy head,
Small quail dart up, through shafting sunlight fled.

Like brightness buried by one's sullen mood
The quail rise startled from the threadbare wood;
A voice, a step, a swift sun-thrust of feather
And earth and air come properly together.

☙ The woods in Missouri on the banks of the Mississippi
through which I used to tramp endlessly as a boy had their terrifying aspects. All around in them were sinkholes left by an
earthquake: at the bottom of each was an overgrown black
hole that I was convinced was a bottomless pit that would
surely swallow me up if I allowed myself to slip into it. As I
went along skirting the sinkholes, I would come at times on a
snake and at other times on a covey of quail. In the absolute
stillness of the autumn woods both were terrifying, but in the
vision of the quail there was not only terror but a haunting
beauty as well. I have tried to put it down in "Quail in Autumn."

I wrote this poem over forty years ago as a college student
and had never published it. Almost every word in it is just as
I set it down with the exception of the first two lines of the
final stanza. When I came on the poem a few years ago (I

never throw any paper away even if it contains only a phrase or two), I found that I had written something like this:

The quail rise startled from the autumn wood,
Love makes its brief appearance as it should.

I realized, of course, that to a young man of twenty love is what always appears, or should appear, at any time of the day or night, but in middle age, I could see that what I had really experienced so long ago—and was still experiencing—was the chilling beauty, the terror, of poetry itself. I hope that I have communicated something of that in my revision of the last stanza.   —W.J.S.

John Updike:
DOG'S DEATH

She must have been kicked unseen or brushed by a car.
Too young to know much, she was beginning to learn
To use the newspapers spread on the kitchen floor
And to win, wetting there, the words, "Good dog!
Good dog!"

We thought her shy malaise was a shot reaction.
The autopsy disclosed a rupture in her liver.
As we teased her with play, blood was filling her skin
And her heart was learning to lie down forever.

Monday morning, as the children were noisily fed
And sent to school, she crawled beneath the youngest's bed.
We found her twisted and limp but still alive.
In the car to the vet's, on my lap, she tried

To bite my hand and died. I stroked her warm fur
And my wife called in a voice imperious with tears.
Though surrounded by love that would have upheld her,
Nevertheless she sank and, stiffening, disappeared.

Back home, we found that in the night her frame,
Drawing near to dissolution, had endured the shame
Of diarrhoea and had dragged across the floor
To a newspaper carelessly left there. *Good dog.*

Joyce Carol Oates:
BACK COUNTRY

From the field behind our house, a low howling.
Slow drawn-out bleats of pain.

It was his boy's dog, therefore his, so he had every right
to grab the .22, and shoot:
his blood-threaded eyes are glazed with piety.

The dog was always hungry, he says.
The dog was in the way, the dog was vicious,
her tail was always slapping his legs.

Now his three children run to us, to hide,
even the fifteen-year-old is crying,
wanting the cellar. And not for the first time.

An August afternoon, very slow.
The first shot missed the heart, flew through the belly,
the second shot evidently went wild,   -
by the third Nellie had fled into the road,
yipping pain in ribbons, bright red confetti,
we had never heard anything like it before.

Our neighbor was too drunk to give chase.
There was no sport to it: he fired again, into the air.
Nellie dragged herself into our yard
where she snapped at my brother.
Howling on three legs she ran to our back field.
And now she is out there, dying.
But it is a noisy procedure.
It is not so easy as one might think.

In the meadow, in sweet clover,
O finally. Finally. An hour and ten minutes by the clock.
We can't call the police, my mother says, we can't make
trouble my grandmother says, they are thinking of our
      neighbor's wife,
they are thinking of the children, and of the gun.

Across the slouching wire fence he shouted words
we could not hear. Not sober but apologetic.
A little frightened. The rifle, the noise, the upset,
the trespass into another's yard.

My father comes home from work and my mother tells him
and he says very little, he goes out to bury the dog,
he doesn't want us with him, and then he goes next door to talk,
it is not for the first time, he talks, our fathers talk,
not for the first time, and then he returns,
his face leaden with disgust,
his skin flushed and mottled.
But he says nothing to us.

These things happen,
dogs get in the way.

Gregory Corso:
NEW YORK CITY—1935

I was 5 years old
It was New York December
Horses pulling wagons
        on icy pavements
As always the obvious horror:
A truck—crash—boom
The horse—blood
        sopping in the snow
                making red ice
I cried
My wet eyes seeing a silent
        twitching horse

And it's driver
   head bowed
      walking slowly
      like the sad Italian peasant
         he was—

Steve Orlen:
BIG FRIEND OF THE STONES

The donkey doctor came covered with rain
And a gift, a picture of Jesus that changed
When you looked, his head seemed to wag.
My father is a good man
With a pinecone for his head—
All summer he chops firewood
When the air is hot, not cold.
I've watched him from the rubbish pit
Where I was playing with a snail.
My father says I will become
The guardian of all God's motions,
Wind and sun and rain, the goat
After the grapes, the grapes,
The bees spinning the useful honey.

But I could not save the donkey.
The day the donkey died, a strange
White peace came over our land
Like the doctor's white hand
Into his vest pocket. My father said
The donkey was a friendly old man
Because he carried his burden over the hills
With the flies in his ears
And the dog at his legs.

The donkey doctor yawned and muttered
And we took the graying carcass out
Though it was tired and could not obey.
Please me, I prayed, big friend
Of the stones. We dragged him down the hill
And buried him beside the poplar tree.

When they left, I knelt and dug
A channel to the great head
And stroked his muzzle. I spoke
A little poem I made up in a dream.
It was cold. A leaf fell on my head.
I sneezed. I pushed the dirt back
Over him and thought, Go to heaven
Where you belong and get yourself cured,

Old favorite of Christ. Behind me
It was snowing on the stream.
Up the hill I saw my father
And the donkey doctor swigging whiskey
From the jug. The door to our house
Was open. The dog slept on the hearth.
I sneezed again and it was winter.

⤳ I like to tell a story when I write a poem. Some of the
stories are true, some not so true. But something in me guides
me to tell all the stories as though they were true, as though
they happened to me—I was there, and I'm no liar. I began
writing "Big Friend of the Stones" from a list of words, some
of which rhymed: *donkey, doctor, came, rain, gift, Jesus,
changed, head, wag* . . . The words set me going on a day
when I had no stories to tell but wanted to tell one anyway.
It's a way of finding out what's on my mind. And once a story
gets going, the characters take over. The speaker of this poem—

a young boy—got established right away, so I just let him keep talking until he ran out. Stories also seem to provide their own endings. Although the method for writing such a poem may be arbitrary, I am responsible for how it sounds and what it means.   —S.O.

Ted Kooser:
CAMERA

It's an old box camera,
a Brownie, the color and shape
of the battery out of a car,
but smaller, lighter.
All the good times—
the clumsy picnics on the grass,
the new Dodge,
the Easter Sundays—
each with its own clear instant
in the fluid of time,
all these have leaked away,
leaving this shell,
this little battery without a spark.

Linda Pastan:
GRAMMAR LESSON

Move into
the past tense
where memory
is negotiable,
where the cold
white house
hammered together
with pain
rocks in the wind
like a cradle.
Choose adjectives
with care: warm . . .
green . . . simple.

Eliminate verbs
of motion.
Finally change
to the plural
where you will
never be
lonely again.

Mike Lowery:
THE SMELL OF OLD NEWSPAPERS IS ALWAYS
STRONGER AFTER SLEEPING IN THE SUN

in the chaos of the autumn sun
I wear old clothes and
sit among other old men
in Owen Park
envying new mothers
with their fixed and
regular lives of
formulas and diapers

and wonder what went wrong
with the curly-headed kid
who played sand-lot ball
with bones that begged for the sun
in the days when scores
were chalked on fences

the fences are still there
but the boy has become nailed
by the sun to time thickened
memories of old games
whose scores are lost forever

191

Images of old newspapers, the sun, sand-lot ball and scores chalked on fences have a way of shaping this poem. These images become the bones gleaming behind the flesh.

I tried to bring to this poem the "wonder of childhood"—by creating the scene of old men sunning themselves while young mothers tend to the needs of their babies. The poem then leaps back toward memory, as Robert Frost said, to "the surprise of remembering something I didn't know I knew."

This poem operates in two time frames. The old man is marking the seasons like everyone else in the park, but he is also "flashing back" to the time when seasons were marked by the games of children.

I hope this poem conveys the impression that maybe, just maybe, the old man is carrying some chalk, just in case.

—M.L.

Richard Snyder:
THE AGING POET, ON A READING TRIP TO DAYTON, VISITS THE AIR FORCE MUSEUEM AND DISCOVERS THERE A PLANE HE ONCE FLEW

There was in danger desperate delight
When I in that ship was a stowaway.
It was primitive, I its proselyte.

Remembering, I give myself a fright
And the plane a pat, which still is to say
There was in danger desperate delight.

Or is that now romantic second-sight?
Machined in deadly earnest, not for play,
It was primitive, I its proselyte.

But, oh, that detachment, that impolite
Aloofness when I was its protégé.
There was in danger desperate delight

Of high, blue pasture through which to excite
By joystick whip a racing runaway.
It was primitive, I its proselyte.

Grounded now, hangered here, she was my rite.
We are survivors to a duller day.
There was in danger desperate delight.
It was primitive, I its proselyte.

〰 My title, which, incidentally, is the longest I believe I ever
appended to a poem, speaks, literally, of how I came to write
this poem: I was in Dayton as a visiting poet in the public
schools, and, while I started my day early, I was finished by
about two in the afternoon; so one day I went to the Air Force
Museum and did discover there a plane I had flown in in WWII.
Its serial number ended in 100, and under the cockpit window
I found a faded "The Century Note," my plane's name. It was
an uncanny feeling, and later in my motel room I tried, on
Howard Johnson stationery, to find words for that feeling, so
to share it, which is what I think all poets do. Later I finished
it in my study at home after the trip. I settled on a French
form, the villanelle, which has the qualities of tightness and
refrains, which effects I wanted. I modeled my villanelle after
one of the rarely successful ones in English, Dylan Thomas'
"Do Not Go Gentle Into That Good Night." The villanelle has
five stanzas of a,b,a and a sixth of a,b,a,a, as well as an alternate refrain of the first and third lines which closes each stanza
and double echoes at the end. A proselyte is a convert, and a
protégé is one who is under the patronage of someone who
influences his career. The twin tensions are my remembered
delight and its attendant dangers.   —R.S.

Jonathan Holden:
ALONE

Alone is delicious.
There's no one to see.
I can eat these low clouds
and the body of wind
that's turning them into rolling
tumbleweed, eat with my hands,
get crumbs over everything,
crumbs of clouds on my nose,
in my fingernails, clouds smeared
all over my shirt and my chin,
I can lick the clouds off my fingers
and no one can see or care if
I have as much dessert as I want.
I just reach into those blue
holes that I've left and pull out
whole fistfuls of sky, of infinity.
It's tasteless and so hard
I can chew it for hours.

Edward Field:
TULIPS AND ADDRESSES

The Museum of Modern Art on West Fifty-third Street
Is interested only in the flower not the bulb:
After the Dutch tulips finished blooming in the garden last
        year
They pulled them up and threw them away—that place has
        no heart.
Some fortunately were rescued and came into my possession.

I kept them all winter in a paper bag from the A & P
At first where I was living then on the Westside
Until the next-door tribe of Murphies drove me out with
    rock and roll,
Then at Thompson Street in the Village where overhead
A girl and her lover tromped around all night on each other.

And that wasn't the end of it: I shlepped those bulbs around
For two months from place to place looking for a home,
All that winter, moving . . . Oy—although this was nothing
    new for me
Coming as I do from a wandering race,
And life with its ten plagues making me even more Jewish.

Now I am living on Abingdon Square, not the Ritz exactly,
    but a place
And I have planted the tulips in my window box:
Please God make them come up, so that everyone who passes by
Will know I'm there, at least long enough to catch my breath,
When they see the bright red beautiful flowers in my window.

Ted Kooser:
CENTRAL

As fine a piece of furniture
as any Steinway, all oak
and nickel and Bakelite,
her switchboard stood in the kitchen,
stretching the truth. While she sat
with her ear to the valley,
rumor reached its red tendrils
from socket to socket, from farm
to farm. When the sun went down,

she sat in the dark. Those voices
she'd listened to all afternoon,
clear as the high, sharp cries of geese,
flew over her house and were gone.
The loose lines buzzed. In the moonlight,
her hands held the wilted bouquets
of pink rubber. "Central," she'd say
to the darkness, "This is Central.
Hello? Is there anyone there?"

∽ Like many of my poems, "Central" is about the past, and like many of my poems, I've written it from memory.

"I remember . . ." How many times has each of you heard those two words? When I was young, they seemed to come from everywhere—from my grandparents, my parents, the neighbors. I got tired of it, and moreover, I felt left out. I was so young that I didn't have any stories like theirs. But I listened, and listened, and listened, and those stories and the way that they told them became a big part of my life. Now I'm old enough to tell stories, and my poems are my stories.

Next to love, storytelling is the best bridge between the generations. We all learn from stories, and we take the truths from these stories and build them into our own lives. "Central" is a story about a woman who ran one of the old-fashioned telephone exchanges in the county where my grandparents lived.

For the first fifty years of this century, give or take a few, every telephone had a personal operator inside, waiting for instructions. Or, it *seemed* as if she was just inside the phone, waiting for you to pick it up. She'd say "Number please," and you'd give her a number, and she'd place the call for you. But she also could listen in on your call, and you always wondered if she was sitting there listening. You had to be careful about what you said to your friends, because there were no sure secrets over the phone lines in those days.

The woman in my poem is one of those operators who has

made it a habit of listening in on the private conversations of others, and who has done her share of gossiping about what she's heard. As a matter of fact, she's built her life around overhearing gossip, and it's gotten to the point that she doesn't have much else. As the poem ends, she's alone in her darkened house, listening into the buzz of the empty wires.

I don't mean for there to be a lesson in this poem, but I suppose one can't avoid having some sort of lesson in a story. I must have chosen to write about this woman for some reason, and it was probably that there seemed to me to be some sort of truth in her story. For our purposes let's just say that people who depend too much upon the lives of others for their own meaning in life can be left alone and empty.

That's my story.   —T.K.

Richard Wilbur:
THE MILL

The spoiling daylight inched along the bar-top,
Orange and cloudy, slowly igniting lint,
And then that glow was gone, and still your voice,
Serene with failure and with the ease of dying,
Rose from the shades that more and more became you.
Turning among its images, your mind
Produced the names of streets, the exact look
Of lilacs, 1903, in Cincinnati,
—Random, as if your testament were made,
The round sums all bestowed, and now you spent
Your pocket change, so as to be rid of it.
Or was it that you half-hoped to surprise
Your dead life's sound and sovereign anecdote?
What I remember best is the wrecked mill
You stumbled on in Tennessee; or was it
Somewhere down in Brazil? It slips my mind

197

Already. But there it was in a still valley
Far from the towns. No road or path came near it.
If there had been a clearing now it was gone,
And all you found amidst the choke of green
Was three walls standing, hurdled by great vines
And thatched by height on height of hushing leaves.
But still the mill-wheel turned! its crazy buckets
Creaking and lumbering out of the clogged race
And sounding, as you said, as if you'd found
Time all alone and talking to himself
In his eternal rattle.
                        How should I guess
Where they are gone to, now that you are gone,
Those fading streets and those most fragile lilacs,
Those fragmentary views, those times of day?
All that I can be sure of is the mill-wheel.
It turns and turns in my mind, over and over.

෨ "The Mill" is a poem about a last conversation with an acquaintance, who died soon after. The talk *actually* took place in a Cambridge bookshop, but in the poem I transferred it to a bar. Why? Because the inching light on the bar-top, with its suggestion of fading time, gave me a scene more in keeping with the theme; also because conversations in bars are likely to be rambling and disjointed, and thus to express the character of life as we live it—jumbled, fragmentary, uncertain as to form and direction. The poet is particularly struck by the anecdote of the abandoned mill; it comes to stand for "time all alone," for time which means nothing because it is not geared to human life. The poet then has another thought: what happens to a man's memories when that man no longer inhabits time? The next-to-last line implies that those memories become as meaningless as the mill-wheel; but the last line, as one good reader of this poem remarked, says that the dead man's fragmentary life has become a part of the turning images of the poet's mind, and is thus momentarily preserved from time and death.

If this poem succeeds, I think it is partly because of the naturalness of its flow—the probability of the situation and of the sequence of thoughts which it provokes. Also because the language, though plain enough, has moments of vividness ("slowly igniting lint") or double meaning ("became you") and because the description of the mill-wheel has an appropriate noise and rhythm.   —R.W.

David Allan Evans:
NEIGHBORS

They live alone
together,

she with her wide hind
and bird face,
he with his hung belly
and crewcut.

They never talk
but keep busy.

Today they are
washing windows
(each window together)
she on the inside,
he on the outside.
He squirts Windex
at her face,
she squirts Windex
at his face.

Now they are waving
to each other
with rags,

not smiling.

Henry Carlile:
LISTENING TO BEETHOVEN ON THE OREGON
COAST

About a quarter to ten the door softly opened
then closed again.
No one was there, no wind outside.
Earlier I'd watched two trawlers miles apart
work past the North Head lighthouse.
When I looked again they were gone.
Only the owl light of the beacon,
the distant whistle of a buoy,
and the surf wild from a storm miles out at sea.
Beyond the window, cliffs fall away in blackness.

There are wrecks out there,
sunken masts slanting up like crosses
on submerged churches,
bones of fishermen that flow away in phosphorus
past yellow eyes of lingcod,
flat ridiculous soles that walk the sea floor
like lost shoes.
Everything there broken, torn down, consumed.
Each tide a regurgitation of casualties
bleached by salt and moonlight.
Walking by night your feet kick sparks from sand,
the night cries of birds drown in the surf's roar.

Edward Field:
UNWANTED

The poster with my picture on it
Is hanging on the bulletin board in the Post Office.

I stand by it hoping to be recognized
Posing first full face and then profile

But everybody passes by and I have to admit
The photograph was taken some years ago.

I was unwanted then and I'm unwanted now
Ah guess ah'll go up echo mountain and crah.

I wish someone would find my fingerprints somewhere
Maybe on a corpse and say, You're it.

Description: Male, or reasonably so
White, but not lily-white and usually deep-red

Thirty-fivish, and looks it lately
Five-feet-nine and one-hundred-thirty pounds: no physique

Black hair going gray, hairline receding fast
What used to be curly, now fuzzy

Brown eyes starey under beetling brow
Mole on chin, probably will become a wen

It is perfectly obvious that he was not popular at school
No good at baseball, and wet his bed.

His aliases tell his history: Dumbell, Good-for-nothing,
Jewboy, Fieldinsky, Skinny, Fierce Face, Greaseball, Sissy.

Warning: This man is not dangerous, answers to any name
Responds to love, don't call him or he will come.

Keith Wilson:
THE IDIOT

Another road. It seems sometimes
all the earth is roads and he stood
by one: flat forehead, bulging
saffronblue eyes, dribbling mouth.

A deformed man-boy, peeing by the road,
clothes torn and filthy, the strength
of a bear in his arms, his bland
peaceful looks, eyes like wells
child eyes how

        I remember his mouth
looselipped, laughing, his dark laughter
the warm rich tones of his joy at the
things he alone saw walking (or riding,
who knows?)

—down the road he stood beside, empty
road, crowds marched for his mind and
who is to tell the stories he saw
flashing in the dust?

Henry Carlile:
DODO

Years they mistook me for you,
chanting your name in the streets,
pointing grubby fingers.
Today in the natural history museum
I saw why.
Dodo, you look the way I feel,
with your sad absentminded eyes
and your beak like a stone-age axe.
Even your feathers
dingy and fuzzy.
What woman would want them for a hat?

With a name like *Didus ineptus*
where could you go,
wings too small to fly with
and feet so large and slow?
You were not very palatable.
Men slaughtered you for sport.
Hogs ate the one egg you laid each year.
Sometimes I think I know how it feels
to be scattered over the world,
a foot in the British Museum,
a head in Copenhagen,
to be a lesson after the fact,
an entity in name only,
and that taken in vain.

⋐⋑ Most of my poems come from personal experience,
though they are seldom strictly autobiographical. A poem, if it
is to live, must make its own declaration of independence, and
it can only do this if the poet adopts a passive role and allows

the poem to say itself. For this reason I try not to have too strong a sense of where I am going when I begin a poem. I try to learn from my own work and let it show me what I need to know. Poetry then becomes a way of clarifying my own experience and perhaps sharing it. If a poem does not do much more than I intended when I began it, it dies on the page and cannot declare itself. My best poems are mysteries to me, artifacts to which I return for instruction, just as any reader might. Beyond having special knowledge about what inspired the poem in the first place—knowledge which may in any final critical estimation be irrelevant—I know little more about my own work than my most perceptive reader. And the reader may know a great deal more. A poet's exegesis of his or her own work may limit as well as illuminate. In the end, three basic rights are at stake: the poet's right to privacy, the poem's right to declare itself, and the reader's right to reasonable interpretation.   —H.C.

Cynthia Macdonald:
CELEBRATING THE FREAK
—for May Swenson

The freak is	the other
The freak is	wrapped in lamb cloth because
It is precious	
The freak is	precious
The freak is	the other
Alarming us	when it talks through the crook in its arm as it has no mouth
Astounding us	when it threads its legless, armless body through the eye of a needle
Amazing us	when it plays a violin concerto with its feet

The German freak	replaces vaccine for the Germans
The Finnish freak	swims the Baltic for the Finns
The Armenian freak	disarms the cruelest Armenians
The Polish freak	is a totem for the Poles
The freak wears	well
Though it dies early	
The freak wears	silk and velvet to promote its nobility
The freak wears	on the outside what we conceal
The freak wears	down. It becomes tired of being
The freak. It retires	to a country home built to its
Freak specifications:	low toilets or moving staircases or
	beds the size of billiard tables
The freak leaves us	bereft, forcing a little
Mutilation somewhere	to set things right
To wreak	penance
To set	the freak flags flying.

Ed Ochester:
IN THE LIBRARY

the silent girl,
the ugly one,
waits out the spring above her books;
her thoughts poise between
pleasures in the strong sun
and the despair her fragile body brings.

She is the white crane
staring downward,
conscious of her reed neck
that the smallest stone can break.

Jonathan Holden:
DANCING SCHOOL

Marcia Thompane was light and compact,
her silk sides slick as fish's scales.
Doing the box step with me, she
stared into space, waiting
for somebody else.

Vernell Peterson was tense, rickety.
I had to crane up to speak
to her face. My fingers clung
to the rungs of her spine. Trying
to lead Vernell in the swing step
was like leading a dogwood tree.

Poor Liddy Morrison was always
the last to get picked. She was dense,
moist. An inner tube was tied
to her waist. Her gauze dresses
rasped like dry grass.
As I neared her, she'd stare
up with a dog's expectant look. I'd try
to be nice, to smile as though
I were glad it was her
I was stuck with; but Liddy
outdid me: she'd pretend
to be grateful.

Margo Lockwood:
DECEMBER ECLIPSE

The birds
confused by the angle
of light during the eclipse
resumed their getting up,
squawking & complaints.

I stood on the beige-grained sidewalk
in my town facing east
and positioned the hardware store's
gingerbread roof between me
and the sun's angle.

Within fifteen minutes
saw the rick-rack become a scalloped jumble
of not exact shadow,
of vague definitions.

The geese or gulls
that headed south all month
along the Beacon Street car-tracks
started to veer and wonder
what was up, their v's wavering

and the sky took on
a veil of gray
with the weaker sun
still flickering
and making motes sunlike,

casting ambiguous shadows
of telephone poles and parking meters
thickened and grayed
on the ground
like totems of fading skywriting.

I hoped like eskimos or hawaiians
my townspeople would run amok

come pouring out of bank and bar
or orgiate on the corner of
Washington & Beacon,

but they must have learnt
in school to stay indoors
when the sun is acting up,
and not look up like Lot's wife
looking back, or smoke a piece of glass
& participate in the cosmos
like a peeping tom.

᭶ I was standing in the corner of my kitchen in December 1976 describing to my four children why birds fall alseep during an eclipse (they think it is dusk!) and I said "they are confused by the angle of light" and a shudder went through me. I turned over a piece of paper that was a shopping list, put it down on the red formica counter, and wrote it out in red magic marker.

I had, about two weeks earlier, been overhearing everyone in my town that morning of the eclipse, bothering and bustling about why you *shouldn't look up nakedly at the sun!* Burnt retinas, blindness, death from sun rays penetrating into the brain—all these warnings made me laugh. The moment the eclipse, proper, began, I had been buying brass screws at my hardware store, mentioned in the poem. Mr. Connelly, the owner, said he had been selling those cardboard periscopes with mirrors, all morning.

I went outside to find the sun, happened it was over the hardware store, at 11:25 in the morning, not at high noon. I decided that if I looked at the sidewalk it would have the shadow of the eclipse.

The geese migration had been taking place from about Thanksgiving on, and I think our trolleyline was part of their natural flyway, as it is a valley between two hills.

The word "totems" in my associative process, which was working at about 295 m.p.h. by that time, led to Eskimos, then Hawaiians, both of whom have a short term insanity caused by pressure of some sort, cabin fever or running amok. My mother loved details about faraway tribal customs and used to tell us lurid anecdotes when I was young, straight from the pages of the "Royal Road to Romance," of Richard Halliburton.

She it was who proofread the poem and chided me on my spelling of the word "amok" which I had spelled phonetically "amuck".

I wrote the poem straight out as it is now, no revision except for probably end breaks of either nouns or verbs, read it through, thought, "Boy, that's a lot of material in one poem"— and just left it on the kitchen counter, typed. That week, a poet who taught my children piano lessons, in exchange for furniture, booze or to take my poetry class, happened to read it on the counter, while he was drinking a cup of tea, during his piano lesson break.

He started roaring with laughter, and said, "Did you make this all up?"

I said with some indignation, "Of course not. It is all true. You can't fake things in a poem like that."

Didn't think of the poem again for years, as it lay in piles of bills and letters, but sent it to *Hanging Loose* when I was thinking of things they might publish, and they liked it. –M.L.

Ralph Pomeroy:
SNOW

Tilt. Wilt.
The gay day dances
down. Drown-
ing, lace flakes
make milk lakes.
Children shout
about the
gone lawn,
catching the ripped-up air
where it walks and
sifts. Drifts,
like dandy dunes,
pack over straw-strewn
roses. Hoses,
lax in their dreams of spring,
sleep deep.

⬤ This is a poem about the sound of words and the experience of a snowfall. It is heavily rhymed—"tilt-wilt", "gay-
day", "shout-about", and so on. These are examples of what is
called "pure" rhyme because they sound so nearly alike. There
are other, "impure" rhymes in the poem, rhymes such as "lace-
flakes" and "gone-lawn" which sound *less* like each other than
the "pure" ones do. Then there are games of alliteration (words
with the same beginning letters), the D's in "day dances down.
Drown-" (which has been broken in two with a hyphen in
order to achieve the rhyme "down-Drown"), the M's in "make-
milk", etc. There are also examples of consonance (similar
sounds at the *ends* of words) like the K's in "make-milk", the
N's in "gone-lawn", and on. Another playful device is the
placement of a word at the end of a line with its rhyme at the

beginning of the next line down—"flakes-make", "shout-about", "air-where".

But this is all just having fun with words to make a poem just the way a composer uses notes to make music. The aim is to delight by making a musical picture or statement about a vivid experience, in this instance the delight of snow falling in someone's yard.   —R.P.

David Allan Evans:
RETIRED FARMER

Maybe he dreamed of
new snow, of shiny handles.

This morning I saw
broom and yellow work-gloves
farm a glittering topsoil
off his porch,
heard on the sidewalk
a scraping, a *ping*
of grain flying
from a shovel.

Then he sat a half hour
in his gray '57 Ford
with the engine warming up,
as if, both hands on the wheel,
he figured he was in motion.

Keith Wilson:
OLD WOMEN BESIDE A CHURCH

the blackshawled women of New Mexico
wait, wait outside their churches, in the
gusty winds, their black dresses

in frail silk & gauze they wait, widows
of Christ, faces stiffly furrowed

cracked to mud they watch, eyes centered
deep in the

      clanging bell

   enter

burn candles for a soul, for
cold beds, flickering oil lights
the wind brushes adobe walls away
grain by grain

⌒⌒ I am what I call a "compulsive" writer—the poems simply come. Afterwards I can *sometimes* figure out why I wrote
them, but almost never why I chose the particular materials I
did. Usually I try to avoid any evaluation of "good" or "bad"
when I am writing or even after. Instead, I try the poems out
on Heloise, my wife, a few trusted friends, and then on an
audience at a reading. I think of myself primarily as an "oral"
poet—am finally most interested in how the poem comes across
in the air, though the trick is always to make it work on the
printed page also. Complicated, I admit.   —*K.W.*

David Ignatow:
PARK

I sit beside old retired Italians.
They chat and have smooth skins.
Their hair is white, and the flesh full.
They make no disturbance.
They rest all day, sitting in a park.
One will come over from his house
and add to the crowd.

They never
grow loud. They talk and laugh,
solid company every day. I love
to come here and sit with them,
I a stranger, and feel the quiet
and stability they make,
and lasting custom.

Mike Lowery:
STROKE

the clock stops ticking
the book slips from my hand

doctors echo in a white room
as I try to think of the word for snow

my life becomes a clean sheet
on an empty bed

I speak in tongues to
captors who carry flowers

I ask for pillows
the nurse brings pudding

Margo Lockwood:
VICTORIAN GRANDMOTHER

In the pinch of time, facing
an upright piano under its
paisley throw

you sport a jet and agate necklace
around your freckled throat.

You were mad for costume jewelry—
and better if it was red,
and soon you ran off
to marry Handsome Jack.

I strain my ears after
your songs, you had a gift
for whistling
with a wild vibrato like a finch;

& people liked to say
while working on potato salad
in the kitchen that old one
about whistling girls & cackling hens—
you showed them.

Whatever else I inherited
I wear a brooch of yours,
a bright wing of a butterfly

fixed under a glass bead—
it's caught there, iridescent & rusty
strung on a knotty silver chain

it carries your memory effortless—
like a sure thing.

Edward Field:
WHAT GRANDMA KNEW

The office feels like a sealed glass case today.
The air conditioning dates from the thirties.
That means it is ten years younger than I am.
Neither of us is working too well.

Outside the summer is going on for the outside world
But time is dragging me unwillingly into winter.
I ask myself my favorite question
"Why must I work for a living?"

This has no answer besides being irrelevant.
Old Italian men are fond of saying "No work, no eat."
And I guess that sums things up,
It says the world is so, and just accept it.

If you're famous, life is fun;
If you're not, you live like others do,
And go to the same death of the heart
Long before the hairs finally all fall out of your head.

If I had banjo eyes I'd strum a tune:
"My grandma always said, Alone is a stone.
But by the time life got through with grandma
She was glad to be alone."

∽ I wrote this poem when I was in my mid-thirties (that
was over twenty years ago). I was working in a trivial but not
too boring office job in Rockefeller Center, stuck in the city in
summer when other people (I imagined) were lounging glam-
orously on the beaches of the world—those others for whom
life was easy. My life, in contrast, seemed a failure. I had neither succeeded in my ambitions as a poet, nor had I found

someone to share my life with. Would it go on like this forever, into old age with its ailments, losing my hair, sitting at the office typewriter, sealed off from life, comparing myself to the rattly old air conditioner installed, probably, when the building was built during the depression (so I was about ten years older than it was).

The one thing I could do was stop working at the business correspondence for a little while and express my feelings in a poem.

Grandma would have made a judgment on my solitary life—No good, Eddie, she'd say. Alone is a stone.

Such wisdom is also no wisdom, because even not alone, with someone, life is no joke either, and Grandma must have learned that after the struggle of raising a family with all the terrible things that happen to dear ones, the disasters—I doubt that she thought the solitary life so bad after all. There's no consolation, no rest, no escape, one way or another, from what life has in store for you. Poor Grandma, she finally took to her bed and stayed there. I would have too, except I had to earn a living—no work, no eat, as I say in the poem.

This jaunty bitter song, tossed off in the midst of a dreary job-day, was a cry from the heart—not a great tragic wail, but a kind of Jewish complaining, and not unaware of its humorous side. It came out of a time in life when it seemed nothing would ever change for me. But it did, shortly after, when my manuscript of poems, which had been rejected about twenty-five times by publishers, won the Lamont Award and was published to critical approval. Then my life changed very much.

But the poem grew out of the static moment before it changed. It was a moment of acceptance of what was (even with the bitterness, the complaining) a giving up fighting against it. Sometimes it takes an acceptance of the circumstances of our life to allow something new to happen, because when you stop resisting, you become empty enough, make room for the new to move in.   —E.F.

Ted Kooser:
IN JANUARY, 1962

With his hat on the table before him,
my grandfather waited until it was time
to go to my grandmother's funeral.
Beyond the window, his eighty-eighth winter
lay white in its furrows. The little creek
which cut through his cornfield was frozen.
Past the creek and the broken, brown stubble,
on a hill which thirty years before
he'd given the town, a green tent flapped
under the cedars. Throughout the day before,
he'd stayed there at the window watching
the blue woodsmoke from the thawing-barrels
catch in the bitter wind and vanish,
and had seen, so small in the distance,
a man breaking the earth with a pick.
I suppose he could feel that faraway work
in his hands—the steel-smooth, cold oak handle;
the thick, dull shock at the wrists—
for the following morning, as we waited,
it was as if it hurt him to move them,
those hard old hands which lay curled and still
near the soft gray felt hat on the table.

Sam Cornish:
WHEN MY GRANDMOTHER DIED

when
my
grandmother
died

a black
bird
was
lost
inside
the
house

Peter Meinke:
ELEGY FOR A DIVER

I
Jackknife swandive gainer twist
high off the board you'd pierce the sky
& split the apple of the devil sun
& spit in the sun's fierce eye.
When you were young you never missed,
archer-diver who flew too high
so everything later became undone.

Later everything burned to ash
wings too close to the sun broke down
jackknife swandive gainer twist
can't be done on the ground
and nothing in your diver's past
had warned you that a diver drowns
when nothing replaces what is missed.

Everything beautiful falls away
jackknife swandive gainer twist
muscles drop and skin turns coarse
even skin the sun has kissed.
You drank the sun down every day
until the sun no longer existed
and only the drink had any force.

Only the drink had any force
archer-diver who flew too high
when you were young you never missed
& spit in the sun's fierce eye.
Later everything burned to ash:
everything beautiful falls away
even skin the sun has kissed
jackknife swandive gainer & twist

II

and now I see your bones in dreams
turning & twisting below our feet
fingerbones bending out like wings
as once again your body sings
swandiving slowly through the stone
that sparks your skull and shoulder bones
layer by layer and over and over
you flash through limestone sand & lava
feet together and backbone arched
like an arrow aimed at the devil's heart
the dead are watching your perfect dive
clicking their fingers as if alive
high off the board & the hell with the chances
once again your body dances
anything done well shines forever
only polished by death's dark weather
diver   diver   diving still
now & forever I praise your skill

☞ "Elegy for a Diver" commemorates a high school friend,
a diving champion in New Jersey, who for various reasons—
perhaps partly the glare of publicity—fell apart: dropped out
of college, got divorced, became alcoholic, died young. The
first part traces his success and downfall, linking him with
mythological/historical figures (Icarus, William Tell), repeating
first the names of his dives, and then entire lines to simulate
the repetitive, cyclic nature of his accomplishments; the second
part, in italics, is a run-on dream sequence celebrating the per-
manence of his victories, preserved in memory and in this poem.
—*P.M.*

Howard Moss:
THE GIFT TO BE SIMPLE

Breathing something German at the end,
Which no one understood, he died, a friend,
  Or so he meant to be, to all of us.
  Only the stars defined his radius;
His life, restricted to a wooden house,
Was in his head. He saw a fledgling fall.
    Two times he tried to nest it, but it fell
    Once more, and died; he wandered home again—
    We save so plain a story for great men.
      An angel in ill-fitting sweaters,
      Writing children naive letters,
    A violin player lacking vanities,
    A giant wit among the homilies—
We have no parallel to that immense
    Intelligence.

But if he were remembered for the Bomb,
As some may well remember him, such a tomb,
  For one who hated violence and ceremony
  Equally, would be a wasted irony.
He flew to formal heavens from his perch,
A scientist become his own research,
  And even if the flames were never gold
  That lapped his body to an ash gone cold,
  Even if his death no trumpets tolled,
    There is enough of myth inside the truth
    To make a monument to fit him with;
  And since the universe is in a jar,
  There is no weeping where his heavens are,
And I would remember, now the world is less,
  His gentleness.

Steve Orlen:
THE AGA KHAN

My Aunt Bebe
Used to visit by surprise
With her husband, Uncle Bob,
A Cadillac convertible and silver
Furs and the thirteen tiny
Carved ivory elephants
Herded into a ring
Given her, she said, by the Aga Khan
Who I imagined rode those elephants
In and out of the ring on her finger.
The summer Bebe lay down
On Mother's bed and moaned
I could see her beauty
Reflected in the mirror
As I stood in the kitchen
Looking in. I saw the scars
Crisscross
Her back and fanny.
After the doctor
Shot her up, she laughed,
Her eyelids fluttering up and down.
Then she sat in the parlor
Playing gin. Father took me out
For a game of catch,
Muttering *morphine,*
Morphine, son of a bitch.
And when
Two years later I saw my mother
All dolled up at the funeral
Kiss my Uncle Bob, lipstick
Streaking across his cheek,
When I saw the draped casket

And the people milling around
I snuck off to the men's room
And tried to laugh
Aunt Bebe's laugh, and wondered
What ever happened to the Aga Khan,
That son of a bitch
Who used to ride those elephants
In and out of the ring,
And what a conqueror he must have been,
Her protector, friend,
On his passage in
And out of that tiny universe
And when would he ever stop?

⌒ "The Aga Khan" is a true story, every word of it—at least it is true so far as I knew when I was a teenager, and so far as I remembered the story twenty or so years later. I had a crush on my Aunt Bebe, because she was beautiful, rich, and unpredictable, a creature outside the limits of my teenage world; she was the first death in my life, and the first person I knew of who was addicted to drugs. I could tell you that I wrote this poem quickly and easily, and that later I changed only a few words. But it is also true that I tried many times over a period of 15 years to write a poem about my Aunt, and I was never satisfied with my efforts. Maybe it took that many years and that many tries for me to finally have some intuitive understanding of her life, her death, my teenage crush, and, probably most important, for me to find the focus of the poem, that clever little ring she wore.   —S.O.

William Stafford:
VACATION

One scene as I bow to pour her coffee:—

Three Indians in the scouring drouth
huddle at a grave scooped in the gravel,
lean to the wind as our train goes by.
Someone is gone.
There is dust on everything in Nevada.

I pour the cream.

⌒ Some people think poetry is artificial, a needless attempt
to impose a form on language. Oh no! What if there is a most
natural, most effective way to say any thing you want to say?
What if you let yourself seek that most natural way, most effective way? The result will be your best language, no matter
how you find it, no matter whether it rhymes or doesn't, and
no matter—to tell the truth—whether it is "correct" or
not . . .

When our train went by a windy, dry place in Nevada, I
saw some people standing by a grave. Just a glimpse, I had—
a piece of life given me and then snatched away. They were so
still, and the wind buffeted them so, and the world stretched
out around them, so lonely—and gone . . .

And we on the train were elegant—warm, easy, ready to
dine. The *form* it all took was just as it came to be in my
poem: a glance out, a crash of dissonant life, and a calm (an
apparently calm) return to our elegance.

But it wasn't the same. But I let the reader or hearer decide
that—with the help of the form.   —W.S.

Henry Carlile:
SPIDER REEVES

But for the broken firing pin
would it have lived elsewhere?
You could have blown it out
with your breath, poked it out
with a stick, but you liked
to see its many eyes gleam
from the chamber
each time you opened it.
The next-door chamber took
in noisy tenants, threw them out.

What the spider thought
of that loud eviction?
It lived next door to death
no more a damned fool than you.
Smokeless powder, Damascus twist?
Lucky you didn't poach your own
head instead of the deer's.
One night you shot at eyes
and fetched a scream so shrill
you thought it was a woman's.

It was a ring-tailed coon's.
Who else but you would plug
a punctured gas tank with a match,
patch a leaking boat with gum,
get lost in fog on an ebb tide
with the wind building?

In school they called you Spider,
not for the spider in your gun,
but because you snagged passes

with your sticky hands
running so many directions at once
it seemed you had eight legs.

Now you run with the tide,
so many lost molecules,
a gleam in the dog shark's eye,
a diatomaceous spark.
You were not very bright.
You could have learned to live.

Richard Snyder:
BLUE SPARKS IN DARK CLOSETS
—for P.T.P., 1896–1975

He is old, two weeks to eighty,
who reads in Greek and Latin
the weighty matins to another day.

He is dying and wants to die
but hates the vespertine light,
so I with the night come to him and stay

to feed him broth and such small news
as 'Andy's ordered his seed.'
But he eschews my need to nourish him.

Hard as this galvanized winter,
he goes about his dying,
imprinter of his last lying on grim

and accepting hospital bed,
nor can think of long-days spring
for himself dead and scattering like chaff.

He recedes into his covers.
I leave him to his leaving
and discover his grieving epitaph

in the closet getting my coat,
when the hanger strikes a spark
to denote by that thin arc his going.

He who knew languages, soil, art,
and music lighted our dark.
We part and mark you, Peter, by our knowing.

Peter Meinke:
DEAR READER

Why don't you write you never
write each day I check the mail
nothing but truss ads & christmas seals
where are you what are you doing
tonight?

How are your teeth?
When I brush mine blood
drips down my chin
are you happy do you miss me
I will tell you
there is no one like you
your eyes are unbelievable
your secrets are more interesting than anyone else's
you had an unhappy childhood
right?

I will rub your feet they're tired
I'll say Hey
let's go to the movies
just the 2 of us
love

peter

Acknowledgments

Permission to reprint copyrighted poems is gratefully acknowledged to the following:

The Antioch Review, for "Letter to a Substitute Teacher" by Gary Gildner, Copyright © 1971 by The Antioch Review, Inc. (first appeared in *The Antioch Review,* Vol. 31, No. 1, Fall, 1971). "Advice to My Son" by Peter Meinke, Copyright © 1965 by The Antioch Review, Inc. (first appeared in *The Antioch Review,* Vol. 25, No. 3, Fall, 1965).

Atheneum Publishers, Inc., for "To Dorothy" from *Star Which See, Star Which Do Not See,* Copyright © 1977 by Marvin Bell, and "What They Do to You in Distant Places" from *These Green-Going-to-Yellow,* Copyright © 1981 by Marvin Bell. Comment on "What They Do to You in Distant Places" Copyright © 1983 by Marvin Bell. "At the Algonquin" from *Second Nature,* Copyright © 1968 by Howard Moss, and "The Gift to Be Simple" from *A Swimmer in the Air,* Copyright © 1957 by Howard Moss. Comment on "At the Algonquin" Copyright © 1983 by Howard Moss.

Best Cellar Press, for "The Gap in the Cedar" from *Accompanied,* Copyright © 1974 by Roy Scheele. Comment on "The Gap in the Cedar" Copyright © 1983 by Roy Scheele.

George Braziller, Inc., New York, for "The Late Mother" from *Transplants,* Copyright © 1976 by Cynthia Macdonald.

Henry Carlile, for "Dodo," "Listening to Beethoven on the Oregon Coast" and "Spider Reeves" from *Running Lights,* Copyright © 1981 by Henry Carlile. Reprinted by permission of the author and Dragon Gate, Inc. Comment on "Dodo" Copyright © 1983 by Henry Carlile.

Carnegie-Mellon University Press, for "The War of the Worlds" and "The World" from *Walking Home from the Icehouse,* Copyright © 1981 by Vern Rutsala. Comment on "The War of the Worlds" Copyright © 1983 by Vern Rutsala. "In One Place" and "The Girl Writing Her English Paper" from *Swimmer in the Rain,* Copyright © 1979 by Robert Wallace. Comment on "The Girl Writing Her English Paper" Copyright © 1983 by Robert Wallace.

William Carpenter, for "Autumn," "Fire" and "The Keeper." Comment on "Fire" Copyright © 1983 by William Carpenter.

Hayden Carruth, for "Mending the Adobe" and "When Howitzers Began" from *Brothers, I Loved You All,* Copyright © 1978 by Hayden Carruth, published by Sheep Meadow Press. Comment on "When Howitzers Began" Copyright © 1983 by Hayden Carruth.

235

Index of poets